THE AUTOBIOGRAPHY
OF THE REV. JOHN JENKINSON

Frontispiece: John Jenkinson, date uncertain. (*Jenkinson family*)

THE
AUTOBIOGRAPHY
OF
THE REV. JOHN JENKINSON

BAPTIST MINISTER
OF KETTERING AND OAKHAM

Edited by
R. L. GREENALL

Victor Hatley Memorial Series
Volume 3

Northamptonshire Record Society
2010

ISBN 978 0 901275 68 4

Published by the Northamptonshire Record Society
Wootton Hall Park, Northampton, NN4 8BQ

*This is the third in a series of paperbacks published to commemorate the life and work of the
late Victor Hatley. Before his untimely death, Victor published articles and booklets on
Northamptonshire and was Hon. Editor of two volumes in the Main Series publications of
this Society. For many years he was a member of the Council.*

Typeset by John Hardaker
Wollaston, Northamptonshire

Printed and bound in Great Britain by Short Run Press Limited
25 Bittern Road, Sowton Industrial Estate, Exeter EX2 7LW

CONTENTS

ILLUSTRATIONS

ACKNOWLEDGEMENTS

Acknowledgements and thanks are owed to Alan Jenkinson of Isham, who first drew attention to the existence of the manuscript "My Life", and to Ann Jenkinson in London, the current owner of the work, who has kindly permitted its publication and rendered much valuable assistance in checking and correcting the transcription. It is some years since I carried out the research for this volume and in thanking the following I am sure that some may be retired, grown old or even passed away. I should like to thank Ann's father, Harold Jenkinson, who years ago sent me valuable information about Jenkinson and his son, Joseph Ashford Jenkinson. Early in his life Joseph Jenkinson moved away from Northamptonshire, but preserved some of his father's papers, notably the manuscript "My Life". My thanks also go to Kathryn Baddiley, a former colleague at Leicester University, who offered to transcribe and type Jenkinson's text, no easy task, but one she accomplished with patience and accuracy.

My thanks are also due to Mrs. S. Mills and more recently Emily Burgoyne at the Angus Library at Regent's Park College, Oxford; the Rev. D. S. Page formerly of Oakham Baptist Church; the Rev. Donald Mackenzie, formerly minister at Fuller Church, Kettering for access to the church archives; the County Archivists and their colleagues at Leicestershire and Northamptonshire Record Offices; to Northamptonshire Library and Information Service and local history librarians at Northampton Abington Street and Kettering Libraries. I also received help and information from the archivist of the Independent Order of Rechabites in Manchester.

INTRODUCTION

It is some years since I first came across John Jenkinson, a Kettering Baptist preacher who led an active public life in the first two thirds of the nineteenth century. I was teaching evening classes in local history in Kettering, and one of the students, the late Frank Thompson, a great collector of Kettering material, gave me a printed pamphlet published in 1829, referring to Jenkinson's part in a painful schism at Little Meeting Baptist Chapel (now Fuller Baptist Church). This resulted in Jenkinson and a group of followers breaking away and eventually establishing their own place of worship. Thereafter, Jenkinson figured frequently in the history of Kettering and places beyond. I began to research his life and build up a picture of the man, his causes and activities. Jenkinson published a fair amount, both in circulated manuscript form and as printed pamphlets, and the contemporary newspapers were a fruitful source of information. It seemed just possible that Jenkinson might have left an autobiography, but none materialised. In the end, I published an article, "Baptist as Radical: the Life and Opinions of the Revd. John Jenkinson of Kettering (1799-1876)", in *Northamptonshire Past & Present*, the annual journal of this Society.[1] As so often happens, shortly after this article was published, news arrived that one of Jenkinson's descendants living in the south of England possessed a handwritten autobiography, a photocopy of which was sent to me through the good offices of Mr. Alan Jenkinson of Isham. Readers who wish to have more background detail on John Jenkinson will no doubt wish to turn to the *Northamptonshire Past & Present* article, but it might be useful for those who do not have ready access to that journal if the main episodes in his life were summarised to provide some clarification of what appears in Jenkinson's "My Life".

Although Jenkinson declared that writing was always "a bore" to him, he was possibly being disingenuous because he rarely seems to have hesitated in taking pen to paper and he had much to say about his life and times. Obituaries and brief lives of notable Baptist ministers often appeared after their deaths, but autobiographies are altogether more rare. Unsurprisingly, in his manuscript account, Jenkinson's religious life and experience are central; there is puritanical soul-searching, theological argument, interpretations of the occasions that Divine Providence apparently came to his aid or smote his enemies, and he itemised the numerous occasions he preached in Baptist chapels in Leicestershire, Northamptonshire, Bedfordshire, and occasionally

---

1 Volume VIII, No.3, 1991-2, pp. 210-226.

farther afield. Writing in retirement, presumably for the benefit of his descendants, Jenkinson was skilled enough not to allow such reflections to grow unduly tedious. But perhaps, above all, what makes his autobiography worthy of publication is not only his busy life as a preacher, but the part he played in local matters and the wider events of his time.

Jenkinson's maternal grandfather was a Baptist minister, but rather than coming to the ministry by the conventional route of a theological college education and training, Jenkinson did it his way – as a largely self-educated young man who found himself the leader of a secession from Little Meeting. Once established in his own chapel, he was welcome as a visiting preacher in other pulpits, though never at Little Meeting, whose members never forgave him (although after sixteen years away from Kettering he and his children did return in 1864). Jenkinson was militant and energetic on several fronts. In his time some Baptist ministers were similarly vehement in their efforts to have the religious and civil disabilities which had lain on Nonconformists since the late seventeenth century removed. This meant opposing the Church of England and its supporters, locally and in Parliament. In Jenkinson's time, the tide of Reform was with the Dissenters, and he played his part in agitating for Reform. More than usually with Nonconformist ministers, Jenkinson identified with the aspirations of the poor and this led him to support Co-operation, Temperance and popular Radical politics from Chartism to the Second Reform Act of 1867.

Jenkinson's story is of a poor boy who made good. He was born in Hallaton, near Market Harborough in Leicestershire. After his father died when Jenkinson was eight years old, his mother and her family were soon impoverished. Jenkinson's schooling (on which he writes informatively) being soon over, he was eventually apprenticed to his great uncle William Stafford, a blind seedsman and market gardener. Jenkinson pays a warm and affectionate tribute to this remarkable man. "My Life", incidentally, explains the transition from Jenkinson's poverty to financial security: to Jenkinson's surprize, William Stafford left him the business. Financially it was Jenkinson's big break in life. His brother Edward joined him in the enterprise.

Their mother being the daughter of the Rev. John Ayer, a Baptist minister, it was perhaps natural that the Jenkinson boys would gravitate to Little Meeting Baptist chapel. Andrew Fuller, whose reputation stands high in Baptist history, was minister. Little Meeting was a major formative influence on John and Edward. There their religious beliefs were developed and their education advanced in the Sunday School, by sermons they heard (and remembered), and discussions in which they participated. Looking back to these years, Jenkinson reflects "at that period the knotty points of Calvinism and Arminianism were much more frequently discussed in the conversations of young persons than now."[2] Kettering was certainly an intensely religious place, known as "the Holy Land" for the strict way the Sabbath was observed and for the high level of church and chapel attendance. It was also a place where Independents and Baptists outnumbered the adherents of the Church of England, and, shortly after the Jenkinsons arrived, Wesleyans established themselves in the town, extending the influence of evangelical religion. At Little Meeting it was a particular source of pride that the Baptist Missionary Society, the first Protestant overseas missionary organisation, was founded there in 1792. Amongst its founders were Fuller and Jenkinson's grandfather. In his autobiography Jenkinson recalls the celebrations when Baptist ministers and lay people from a wide area came to Kettering for the Society's Jubilee celebrations in 1842.[3]

At the Chapel, the young Jenkinson honed his talents. He had a taste for theological argument, knew his Bible backwards and became a formidable reasoner. Just as importantly, he began to preach the gospel at open-air meetings in local villages. Eventually he was admitted as a member at Little Meeting and was baptized by immersion. When Andrew Fuller died in 1815 his successor was the Rev. John Keen Hall, a nephew of the Rev. Robert Hall, a leading Leicestershire minister. It was never going to be easy to follow in Fuller's footsteps; from the start Hall had a minority in his congregation who found him not to their taste. In time, Hall's critics suggested that the precocious Jenkinson be invited to preach in the chapel, which Hall vehemently opposed. In 1824 Hall called for, and won, a vote of support from chapel members. Jenkinson and fourteen others left. Shortly after, Ebenezer Calvinistic Chapel was launched, and Jenkinson became the minister. In his account, Jenkinson does not go into great detail on the secession, and only briefly alludes to the bitter recriminations. Jenkinson seems to have put the matter behind him and got on with making a go of Ebenezer. At Little Meeting, Hall loyalists never forgave Jenkinson and Ebenezer's

2 At the end of the 18th century Baptists in Leicestershire and Northamptonshire were divided into Particular and General Baptists. Particular Baptists were Calvinists, embracing the theology of John Calvin, (who died in 1564), whose main tenet was that Christ did not die for all men, but for the particular Elect, whom God had chosen. Their salvation was *predestined*. General Baptists held to the teaching of the Dutch theologian, Jacob Arminius or Harmesen (who died in 1609), who argued that predestination is "conditional", and that potentially Christ died for all men. At the time Jenkinson was young, Arminianism was in decline but still much discussed.

3 For the background to developments in Kettering, see R. L. Greenall *A History of Kettering*, 2003, chapter 6.

admission into the Northamptonshire Baptist Association. The affair defines what Jenkinson was, a self-made Baptist irregular. Doing it his way never worried him. With occasional days of doubt, Jenkinson possessed formidable self-belief. Nineteenth century Kettering was always a home for "the Awkward Squad" and Jenkinson was a worthy member.

The cause of establishing and building Ebenezer, exercising pastoral care, and, in the process, becoming well known as a preacher, dominated Jenkinson's life for almost twenty years. It was crowned by the extinguishing of Ebenezer's debts in 1843, an occasion for rejoicing. By then Jenkinson had widened his activities considerably. One of the features of his life was that he tried to improve the lot of Kettering's artisans and labouring poor, suffering in the prolonged economic depression of the time. Their sufferings were particularly acute as a result of the collapse of worsted weaving and the chequered economic fortunes of the silk industry established to replace it.[4]

In doing so, Jenkinson became a public figure. He took up journalism, projects for educational improvement, Co-operation, Temperance and Radical politics. The difficulties in disseminating ideas and information to those too poor to buy newspapers led him to start a handwritten "Kettering Magazine", which he produced every month from 1829 until 1848 (two hundred and forty numbers in all). It was a *Tit-Bits* for Calvinists. Starting as a vehicle for religious homilies, it broadened its appeal with short articles on politics, poems, and snippets of information on a variety subjects. Copied and circulated by hand, the Magazine found a readership, though how wide is not clear. In the 1840s, Jenkinson was also involved in *The Citizen*, a penny monthly, the men behind which were Thomas Waddington and Keen Hall's successor at Little Meeting, the Rev. William Robinson. *The Citizen* has claim to be Kettering's first newspaper, but did not survive long (1844-45 and 1846-47). The first newspaper to make any impact was Waddington's weekly *Kettering Free Press*, which appeared after the repeal of "the Taxes on Knowledge" (government duties levied on newspapers designed to suppress Radical ideas) in 1855.[5]

Another form of Jenkinson's literary output was his verses, which first appeared in printed handbill format (See Appendices 3 and 5). Such

4 For the question of the suffering of the unemployed and the problems of poor relief, *see* S. A. Peyton, ed., *Kettering Vestry Minutes AD 1797-1853*, Northamptonshire Record Society, 1933. See also R. L. Greenall *Kettering*, chapter 7.

5 It started as a two-penny weekly the *Kettering Free Press, Northamptonshire Advertiser and Charles Knight's Town & Country Newspaper*. Faced with competition from older Northampton papers, it eventually re-established itself in Leicester as *The Midland Free Press*, where it prospered. It continued to report Kettering news.

pieces were very much part of the Sunday School didactic moralising tradition, and if they do not appeal to the modern mind, Jenkinson's ability to write rhyming couplets seems to have been appreciated by his contemporaries. His most ambitious venture in verse was *Isabel, or The Ghost of Barton Bridge, A Tale of the Fifteenth Century*, the first version of which appeared in the Kettering Magazine in 1847. It was later republished, in instalments, in the *Kettering Free Press* in 1855. It is a long poem consisting of some 298 four-line stanzas in thirteen parts. No one can say Jenkinson lacked literary stamina, but *Isabel* is an example of what could happen when Calvinist morality, local history and Early Victorian medievalism combined. It is the story of the beautiful and virtuous daughter of Lord Latimer of Braybrook, lewd priests and violent noblemen. Isabel is drowned by Barton Bridge and her ghost comes back to haunt the wicked Lord Seagrave, who, in the end, repents and enters a monastery.

Jenkinson's involvement in new social movements is illustrated by his adoption of Co-operation and Temperance. In the later part of the nineteenth century, with Kettering Industrial Co-operative Society (the K.I.C.S.) and four productive Co-operative enterprises, the town became, in the words of one writer, "The very Mecca of Co-operation". But Co-operation had hard times to pass through before the K.I.C.S. achieved success. In 1829 Jenkinson was the leading spirit in the setting up of the first Co-operative Society, which, although it apparently survived for a number of years, has left little evidence of its activities (See Appendix 2).

Temperance, or rather Teetotalism, a movement which originated in the USA and arrived in Britain in the 1820s, was another of Jenkinson's life's causes. At first, he was inclined to criticize total abstention from alcohol as "unreasonable and unscriptural", but in December 1839 he explained in the Kettering Magazine why he had finally come round to accepting it. Thereafter, describing himself as "Baptist and Temperance preacher", he devoted much energy to addressing a great number of meetings on the subject. He was one of the founders of Kettering Temperance Society; for him, forswearing drink was both God's work, constituting a moral re-birth for individual adherents, and a viable social strategy to save the poor from the evils of alcohol. Jenkinson also involved himself in the Independent Order of Rechabites, the first Temperance Friendly Society, which, from its establishment in 1835, spread across the country. Rechabitism took Jenkinson beyond Kettering. In 1849 he was elected "High Chief Ruler" of the Order, taking the chair at its annual Conference. Together with preaching the Word, Temperance was Jenkinson's most abiding concern.

In his time in Kettering, Jenkinson was much involved in politics, particularly where religious issues were involved. Dissenters were first energised in 1828, when he was twenty-nine, by the agitation to repeal the Test and Corporation Acts. These had been designed to exclude or marginalize Nonconformists from the professions, local government and Parliament, and had effectively done so. The great agitation of 1830-32 for a Reform Bill, saw Jenkinson politically active for the first time, and Reform gave political Dissenters further opportunities. The 1835 Municipal Corporations Act (which abolished a great many old borough corporations) was, in places such as Northampton, Leicester and many other towns, a charter for Dissenters to stand for election to borough councils and for the first time play their part in civic government. But not in Kettering, which had never had borough status, and was not to achieve it until 1913. The town, however, now became the polling place of the new North Northamptonshire parliamentary constituency and successive election contests gave Kettering's Dissenters (overwhelmingly Whig or Radical) the chance to witness and participate in election contests.

There were other issues on which Dissenters could focus, which involved battling the Church of England and the Conservative Party, the Church's shield and defender. On such matters as opposing compulsory church rate, the refusal of Anglican clergy to allow Nonconformist ministers to conduct burials in parish churchyards and the monopoly of the Church of England over primary education, Dissenters went on the offensive. In these matters, Jenkinson often found himself allied with Hall's successor, the militant William Robinson. If socially they were not close and differed over certain theological points, they fought together, using the columns of *The Citizen* to appeal to their supporters. In 1834 a British School was opened, which removed the children of Dissenters from the Church's older-established National school. On the matter of funerals of Dissenters, Jenkinson, as his autobiography relates, notably fought the vicar of Isham. With Robinson, he also gave a support to The Society for the Promotion of the Disestablishment of the Church of England, which Dissenters referred to as the "Anti-State Church Association" or the "Liberation Society". Another anti-Church issue was resisting church rate, a parish tax to fund repairs to the parish church. This was an ancient tax, which the incumbent could legally invoke; whenever, that is, he could persuade the parish vestry to accept that he had a case. The vestry would then levy a rate and all rate-payers were liable. Dissenters had to pay, or resist. Before the 1840s, in general, only Quakers refused to pay, and faced the legal consequences of being taken to court and having their goods distrained to pay their rate. In Jenkinson's time, militant Baptists, Independents and Quakers, in places where they were numerous enough on the ground, such as Kettering, organized resistance. Jenkinson, as his autobiography recounts, resisted and had to suffer the consequences. In the end, a truce was established between the rector and moderate Dissenters. It was agreed that if the rector did not call for a *compulsory* rate, Dissenters would make *voluntary* contributions. Principle was upheld; militancy faded. However, it was not until 1868 that Parliament finally abolished church rate.

As well as the politics of religion, Jenkinson became deeply involved in Chartism, a working class movement to persuade (or force) Parliament to accept demands for the six points of the People's Charter. From 1837, Jenkinson was a member of the Kettering Radical Association, serving as treasurer and chief publicist. In 1839 he produced a summary of the Chartist demands in a pamphlet: *Our Rights: or, the Just Claims of the Working Classes, Stated in a Letter to the Rev. T. H. Madge, Curate of Kettering* (summarized in Appendix 4). There had been an incendiary incident in the town and in defending themselves from being involved, the Chartists had referred to their "just rights". Madge queried what these "just rights" were and Jenkinson went into print to inform him. Characteristically, to the customary six points of the People's Charter, Jenkinson added another four, including the demand that the Church should be wholly separated from the State and a total repeal of the New Poor Law, opposition to which was a major factor in the rise of Chartism. Two years before, he had gone into print with *A Letter to the Rev. George Bugg, A.B. Curate of Desborough, Northamptonshire, containing a Summary of the Principles, Objects, and Means of Radicalism*. Bugg had denounced a deputation from the Radical Association who had waited on him as "a set of villains, vagabonds and persons who would not hesitate to plunder their neighbours".

Jenkinson was more involved in Chartist politics than he admitted in his autobiography. Characteristically, after the setbacks of 1839 and 1842, he went off on a tangent of his own, advocating Chartist Temperance as the way forward. He also became interested in the so-called "New Move", an attempt to adopt a programme that would unite Chartists with middle-class Radicals such as Joseph Sturge, the Birmingham banker. Mainstream Chartists rejected the New Move. It was his Radical activities as well as his position as a Baptist preacher that led to Jenkinson being invited to a conference of "Ministers of All Denominations" in Manchester, organised by the Anti-Corn Law League. There he stayed under the roof of Richard Cobden, the League's principal intellectual. Whether through those contacts, or for other reasons, from 1848 Jenkinson was less involved with Chartism than other matters. "My Life" says more about fighting church rate, and for Temperance and Rechabitism than the last hurrah of the Chartist movement.

Accused by opponents of being a "Leveller", Jenkinson rebuffed the charge. What he was, he wrote in *The Citizen*, was an "elevator". "What are elevators? Genius and talent are elevators, knowledge is an elevator, the printing press is an elevator, the schoolmaster is an elevator, Temperance Societies, Mechanics Institutes and Mutual Instruction Societies are elevators. Industry, honesty and amiableness of disposition are elevators." Finally, "Christianity is the most potent and certain elevator."[6]

Jenkinson took an interest in Kettering's local government. He was always anxious to defend the interests of the small property owners. In 1848 this led him into opposition to those people who wanted to secure a local Act of Parliament to make the owners of cottage properties liable for the payment of poor rate, from which they had hitherto been exempt. By that time Jenkinson had invested in twenty-one cottage properties. Jenkinson spoke against the proposed Bill and, under the *nom de plume* A RATE-PAYER, drafted a handbill, *Thirty-One Reasons for Objecting to the Kettering Small Tenements' Rating Bill* [See Appendix 6]. This opposition failed; the Act was duly obtained, and from then on, *owners* of cottage property instead of their tenants had to pay the poor-rates. In local government matters, Jenkinson was long to remain a stalwart of the "Economiser" position. As such, his day was to come. From the later 1850s the small-ratepayer alliance in Kettering success-fully frustrated "Progressives" for some years, during which the sanitary state of the town worsened.

In 1848, Jenkinson's life took on a new direction. In November he accepted an invitation to become Baptist minister at Oakham, Rutland, whence he moved the following June. Although he never lost touch with what was happening in Kettering and remained close to his brother Edward, who carried on the market gardening business, for the next fifteen years Kettering ceased to be his main sphere of activity. Oakham was only twenty miles away and Jenkinson paid occasional visits, but Kettering rather forgot him. He did not forget Kettering and, when the time came for him to retire, he was happy to return, declaring that he would never again leave. He said he was resolved to die there, and so he did.

One reason why Jenkinson moved was that, by then, he was married with a growing family and in need of a more settled income than he had from Ebenezer. The offer of £52 a year from Oakham was substantially better than the modest stipend from Ebenezer. He recalled that he first cast eyes on Selina Ashford, the daughter of the Rev. Joseph Ashford, a Baptist minister, in 1838. They married in Northampton

6 *The Citizen*, No. 2, 1st August 1846.

Registry Office in 1843. Jenkinson, who in old age remembered that he had tried and failed several times to enter the happy state of matrimony, was then forty-four. By the time he moved from Kettering, he and his wife had three children, Emily, Laura and Joseph Ashford; three more were to be born in Oakham.

Another reason may well have been that his time at Ebenezer had run its course. By 1848 his band of original supporters was dwindling through old age and death, and he sought pastures new, although there was no decline in chapel membership. After Jenkinson left, his brother Edward took responsibility for the running of Ebenezer. For about a year a Welsh Dissenting Minister filled the post, but the income from voluntary offerings was inadequate and worsened as his relationship with his hearers became difficult. After Reynolds, there were others but none stayed long. Edward tried to keep the cause alive, but he died in 1858. Yet Ebenezer struggled on, Jenkinson returning to preach one last time in 1863. The following year the building came into use as a boot and shoe warehouse.

Jenkinson also moved to Oakham because it offered him a more secure status. As he put it, "I was now, of course, a member of the North-amptonshire Baptist Association into which we had in vain sought admission six years before." The unforgiving hostility of Little Meeting Baptists had blocked Ebenezer's acceptance. Oakham, on the other hand, carried automatic membership of the Association. It is also possible that Jenkinson quit Kettering over the passing of the Kettering Small Tenements Rating Act, although he was still liable for rates levied on his cottages.

In a wider context, 1848-49 marked the end of an era. Chartism had shot its bolt; as the economy improved the prospects for Reform faded. The next decade and a half contained fewer excitements. Politically, Jenkinson moved in a different Radical direction. He took up the Anti-Corn Law League cause of trying to promote International Peace and understanding in reaction to Palmerston's belligerent foreign policy. In 1855 he published *Does Christianity Sanction War?* and the Peace Society subsequently engaged him to give propaganda lectures. In the year commencing April 1862, he gave no less than forty-two on a circuit which took in Rutland, Leicestershire, parts of Lincolnshire and Northamptonshire. All that travelling and speech-making in his early sixties is a testament to his stamina. However, apart from his *The Universality and Unchangeableness of Jehovah's Laws* (1860), Jenkinson did not go into print much in his Oakham years. On the Temperance front, he remained active, and regular invitations to preach or give general talks on subjects such as "The Wit and Wisdom of Women", "The

Winds" (see Appendix 7) and "The Chemistry of Ordinary Things", still came his way. He seldom declined an invitation. The *Northampton Mercury* (6 February 1858) briefly reported a lecture of his, "On the Faculty of Observing", given in Wellingborough in 1858. "The lecture abounded in practical remarks, given with an epigrammatic terseness and humour which reminded us of Franklin. It was well-received."

As a minister, Jenkinson led a busy pastoral life. Under him the Baptist cause in Oakham and district prospered. Chapel membership grew, and by 1852 the building needed to be enlarged. Outreach chapels and a Sunday school were restored or newly opened in nearby Langham and Braunstone. One of the things close to his heart was the formation of a Meeting for Rutland of "Ministers of Different Denominations", modelled on one in Northamptonshire. Regular meetings were held in which papers were read and discussed, and these forged stronger bonds between Baptists, Independents and Methodist Reformers. For these ministers, there were also regular meetings of the Bible Society and the Religious Tract Society to support.

In Oakham, Jenkinson involved himself in certain local government matters, principally over a new cemetery when the parish churchyard was closed to further interments. For Dissenters, it was important that the new Burial Board should be made up of laymen rather than clergy, a struggle in which Jenkinson played a part. Their list of names was the one the parish agreed to. In more secular matters, when a Literary Institute was founded in the town, Jenkinson was a strong supporter and was always happy to deliver one of his lectures when invited.

Jenkinson's family grew in Oakham. His daughters Mary Selena and Louisa were born there and a second son, Albert Henry, arrived. He, alas, was sickly and died a year later. Following this last pregnancy, Jenkinson's wife's health began to fail, and to the family's sorrow, she died in 1856. Her mother and father, who had bought a house in Oakham to be near them, were also dead by then. The unexpected death in 1858 of his brother Edward, with whom he had always been close, was another blow. Yet, despite these sorrows, family life had its enjoyable episodes. Jenkinson records a visit with his wife and father-in-law to the Great Exhibition, and there was a memorable family excursion to Matlock Baths, and a seaside holiday in Scarborough.

After fifteen years, Jenkinson left Oakham. As he remarked, it was a fortunate Nonconformist minister who enjoyed unbroken amity with his congregation. Baptists could be curmudgeonly. Jenkinson's contentment was upset by a confrontation with his critics, in which an incident in his private conduct was called into question. On this he supplies few details, and although he triumphed over his opponents, it soured him. In 1864, in his sixty-fifth year, he resigned and moved back to Kettering.

If Jenkinson envisioned a quiet retirement, enlivened with occasional duties as supply preacher and lecturer, it did not quite work out like that. Happy to return to his original "circuit" of Baptist chapels in East Northamptonshire and Bedfordshire, he worked as hard as ever, preaching in aid of chapel restorations, presiding at Sunday school anniversaries, speaking at Penny Readings and other gatherings. In addition, he was persuaded to take on the duties of pastor of the small Baptist chapel at Stanwick, although he insisted on living in Kettering. In Temperance matters he remained as committed as ever.

In politics, Reform was back on the national agenda. As early as August 1861 Jenkinson took part in a Reform meeting in Kettering and prospects advanced more rapidly when Palmerston, the main obstacle to a new Reform Bill, died in 1865. Political Nonconformists took their place in the alliance which came together in Gladstone's Liberal Party. In 1866 and 1867 Jenkinson was much involved in the revived agitation for Reform, affirming his long-held belief in the need for manhood suffrage. It was like going back thirty years, finding that the Radicalism of his Chartist years was still burning bright. Disraeli, briefly prime Minister in 1867, astonished everyone, not least those in his Conservative Party, by passing the Second Reform Act which widened the franchise for working men. When Gladstone became Liberal Prime Minister the following year, his government proved to be one of the most reformist in the nineteenth century, giving the Dissenters much of what they had been agitating for since 1828. Church rate was abolished, as were University Tests, the Church of Ireland was disestablished (on which Jenkinson spoke at public meetings) and Nonconformists warmly endorsed the Education Act of 1870, which brought in the Board School system.

In local government matters, Jenkinson had one last success. The small ratepayers successfully defeated an attempt by Progressives to bring Kettering under a Local Government Board. As a speaker and drafter of handbills (see Appendix 9) Jenkinson was active. "My Life" records the defeat of their opponents in a poll of the parish in 1868, and the presentation of a silver rose to their leading light, George Eldred, a Kettering auctioneer and wine and spirit merchant.

In these years, there was some pleasure and much sadness. In July 1867 he took his family to the great Paris Exposition, a bigger adventure then than now. But the following year, Laura his second eldest child, twenty-two years of age, died of that scourge of the time, tuberculosis. Two years later, in May 1870, his younger daughter, Louisa, died at the age of eighteen. Finally, in 1871, Jenkinson himself suffered the stroke which ended his "public labours". He died on the 11th January 1876.

In his will, he left to his daughter Emily, wife of the Rev. George Roughton, Baptist minister of Watchet, Somerset, his house in Kettering and ten copyhold cottages in Northall. To his son, Joseph Ashford Jenkinson, eight cottages in Prospect Place, the freehold house late belonging to Laura Jenkinson, deceased, two copyhold cottages in Northall and two acres of garden and a barn, "now in the occupation of John Jenkinson" (his nephew, the son of his brother Edward). Joseph was then studying at Regent's Park Baptist College, London, although he subsequently abandoned his course. To Mary Selena, his other surviving daughter, he left a freehold property in Prospect Palace. To his younger brother, Christopher, he left 19 guineas. To Avis, widow of his brother, Edward, £10, the rest going to his son, Joseph Ashford, and to his daughters, Emily and Mary Selina in equal portions. The value of probate was sworn under £450.[7]

Mary Selina did not long survive her father. In April 1877 she married the Rev. Richard Barron, a missionary, at Canonbury Congregational Church in London, and left immediately for Madagascar. Just over a year later she died of typhoid; not the first, nor the last in a line of Kettering Protestant missionaries to die in the field.[8] Her brother Joseph had an altogether longer life, living until 1931. After he left Regent's Park College, he sold up his interests in Kettering, married, and became a teacher, opening a private school on the outskirts of Sheffield. A decade later he moved to London, where he and his family lived in Peckham. He was a good linguist, speaking several languages, and, possibly through his father's friendship with Thomas Cook of Leicester, (who, before he went into the excursion business, was a Baptist preacher, printer and Temperance advocate) was employed for many years as foreign correspondent of a London cutlery firm. Joseph Jenkinson seems to have inherited some of his father's intellectual abilities and antiquarian interests, though not perhaps his religious views or passion for Temperance.[9]

In his particular corner of England, John Jenkinson was a public figure whose life can be reconstructed in some detail. Few autobiographies

7 Northamptonshire Record Office, Peterborough Wills, Register 19, p.118.
8 NRO, Kettering Miscellaneous File, letter from the Rev. George Roughton, Warminster, 10th June 1892.
9 Letter from Harold Jenkinson of Chetnole, Somerset, to Alan Jenkinson of Isham, 11th December 1994.

give a clearer account of the life of a Baptist Minister. Although temperamentally an individualist, he can rightly be seen as representative of that strain of militant Nonconformity which fought the religious and civil disabilities that lay upon Dissenters, and lived long enough to see them largely lifted. What perhaps makes him more interesting than the usual minister is the range of his interests. In what was very much a face-to-face society, his sermons, lectures, journalism and other writings satisfied a contemporary demand. Baptists and others were hungry to hear him speak on religion, Temperance and secular topics. Jenkinson's political activities in particular ensured him a place in the public discourse of his time.

Although Jenkinson's account of his life has much of interest for students of Nonconformity and local history, it is not a literary masterpiece. He failed to reflect in a considered way on his life's experiences, although this is more marked after 1849 than in his earlier account. His general approach, as it is bound to be in an autobiography, was basically chronological. But from 1850 the information becomes more sparse, largely a list of preaching appointments and other events year by year, with less detail than hitherto. He seems to have written it after he retired and clearly he was becoming more tired the longer it went on. If Jenkinson felt that his life to 1848 was the most interesting and exciting part of it, he was surely right. Yet if his writing becomes rather less readable, the listing of his activities is still of value in giving us an account of the busy life of a Baptist preacher. Unsurprisingly (being a Baptist) there is little humour in what he writes, precious little irony and more than a little self-righteousness (the besetting sin of the righteous). The speech he gave in Northampton in 1866 (Appendix 8) indicates that there was more humour in his public lectures and speeches than in his writing.

There is much to admire in Jenkinson. Intellectually and physically, he was remarkably vigorous. One cannot but be impressed by his enjoyment of travel, and if he never seems to have wanted to or been rich enough to own a horse, he was a prodigious walker. His account of going to preach at Brackley, then deciding the next day to walk on to Oxford, tour the colleges, and return to Kettering on foot reveals remarkable physical energy. And there are scenes which this writer, for one, would have liked to have seen; Jenkinson, like some latter-day John the Baptist, immersing converts in the brook at Geddington, his face-off with the constable of Deenethorpe and his intervention in the burial of a Nonconformist child in Isham churchyard. It might be wrong to overstate the importance of John Jenkinson, but he was definitely a man of his cloth, his time and his place.

"MY LIFE" AND OTHER WRITINGS
OF THE REV. JOHN JENKINSON

Figure 1. The leather-bound volume of My Life by John Jenkinson.
(*Ann Jenkinson*)

Notes on Editing

"My Life" is written in a small cash-book, the pages of which measure 7 inches by 4 (171mm x 101). The writer numbered the pages 3 to 311. In the text, where Jenkinson begins a new page, his page number is indicated within square brackets thus, [120]. Occasionally, the writer refers back to an earlier page, and the reader should note that this is a page number in the original text and not the number of a page in this publication. Footnotes have been inserted where appropriate, but occasionally Jenkinson used an asterisk and provided his own note. These have been retained in that form.

The account is written in a small, neat hand, which becomes more crabbed as the writer aged. Punctuation is occasionally biblical, with frequent use of semi-colons, and there is a certain amount of abbreviation. Where necessary, abbreviations have been expanded, capitals raised or lowered, and punctuation altered where modern usage seems appropriate. These apart, the text is as written by Jenkinson.

Apart from the original title, the text of the MS has no chapter or other sub-headings until the year 1850. From that point, Jenkinson inserted the date of each year as a heading. To make the text more comprehensible and readable the editor has inserted sub-headings set in bold italics and square brackets. After "My Life", a selection of Jenkinson's other writings and activities is provided in Appendices.

MY LIFE

[*Early Days: Hallaton and Kettering*]

[3] I have neither the opportunity nor the wish to be proud of my descent. It is true I have some reasons for believing myself to be a descendant of King Adam, the first human sovereign of the whole earth, and also of King Noah, the second universal monarch, but these facts present small ground for pride, inasmuch as the first named by his folly lost his dignity and his possessions, and thus reduced his posterity to poverty and degradation, and the second, like large numbers of his offspring, deeply stained his character with the juice of the grape. Happily, however, relationship to the second Adam more than restored the ruin occasioned by the first, [4] and to be a child of Noah's God is an insufficiently higher honour than that of being a descendant of that distinguished patriarch.

My father, Stephen Jenkinson claimed to be a descendant of a landed proprietor in Derbyshire, and about eighteen months after my birth he and his eldest brother (the grandfather of Mr. S. Pollard of Kettering) took some steps towards obtaining a legal recognition of their right to the estate (which had become the marriage portion of Mrs. Tibbitts of Barton Seagrave, ancestress to the present Viscount Hood), the only results of which were waste of money, loss of time, and the giving the name of Lettice to my only sister, a Lady Lettice Jenkinson having been a former proprietor of the estate, but betwixt whom and ourselves they were unable to discover the necessary links of connection. And no wonder, inasmuch as subsequently for a different purpose I traced the lineage of our family in the parochial register of Hallaton [4] for considerably more than two centuries past.

[5] My dear and honoured mother, (who died at Kettering on September 25th 1863, in the 88th year of her age) was a daughter of the Rev. John Ayer, who at the time of her birth was pastor of the Baptist church at Walgrave, and was subsequently one of the twelve founders of the Baptist Missionary Society. The Ayers were for centuries owners of a farm in Kettering. The dwelling-house in which I now live occupied part of their premises, my study window opens into what was their farmyard and immediately before it is the freestone chimney of what was part of their farmhouse. The site of my house has I believe belonged to our family for at least three hundred years.

About the year 1766 my grandfather John Ayer (who was not then in the ministry) married his cousin Elizabeth, eldest daughter of

John Stafford, who was the youngest of a family of ten children born at Brixworth, near Northampton, in which village their father died of smallpox in 1712: about [6] twenty years after which event, John, being then a young man, came to Kettering Statute Session, where he was hired as a servant to Mr. Nunneley, whose farmhouse was at the back of the *Old White Horse* public house – Mr. Nunneley was ancestor to the Nunneleys of Leicester, Harborough and Boston. After living six years with Mr. Nunneley, John Stafford married the daughter of John Ayer (my grandfather's grandfather). This elder John Ayer was grandson to the Ayer who having influenced his father to sell him a strip off their farmyard, erected the house now occupied by my nephew John Jenkinson. The farm, farmhouse and remainder of the farmyard were a few years subsequently sold by a profligate member of the family to the Duke of Montague, ancestor of the Duke of Buccleuch and Queensberry, to whom they now belong.[10]

My father lived and died at Hallaton in the county of Leicester. He [7] was a boot and shoemaker, having usually about four journeymen and apprentices in his employ. He was in many respects a very ingenious and energetic man, though some times more enterprising than provident. It was from him I derived my first knowledge and my ardent love of arithmetic, of which he also was very fond. His marriage to my mother was celebrated in Kettering parish church in the first week of July 1798. I was the eldest of their four children.

I was born at Hallaton on June 7th, 1799. My father's sister (Mary Jenkinson) kept a grocer's shop adjoining to our house. I have often heard her say what a beautiful child I was, and what marvellous feats I performed in the first three or four years of my life, but myriads of maiden aunts have said the same of their nephews, and especially of those who happened to be the first to whom they sustained the relation of aunt.

[8] My earliest recollection is of a surgeon coming to our house to inoculate me and my sister with the smallpox, which event occurred I believe in the close of 1802. I well remember screaming out, and resolutely refusing to be "cut" until after my sister, and then when I saw the lancet stained with blood I more resolutely refused to be cut at all. Happily, however, I was compelled to undergo the dreaded operation, and have now though a long life derived advantage therefrom, inasmuch as, in visiting persons fearfully afflicted by that terrible disease, I have felt myself comparatively safe from the malady.

10 The Duke was joint lord of the manor of Kettering and a major property owner.

I very distinctly remember the birth of my brother Edward on February 13th 1803. I recollect being dressed on that morning long before daylight: and when I was permitted to see my mother my hands being very cold she put them under her bedclothes, thus exciting a sensation of warmth so delightful [9] that I shall never forget it.

I have no remembrance of learning to read. My earliest reminiscence on that point being that of standing up to read in the first class of a dame's school to which I went, and giving great pleasure to her by being able to tell the number of the verse we were reading, my classmates, some of whom were twice my own age, being unable to say what the figures 27 denoted. As I left her school when five years old, this must have occurred in my very early life.

I then began to attend what is called Hallaton Free School, a scantily endowed charity school held in a miserably low schoolroom into which ninety five boys were sometimes crowded. Mr. James Buzzard was their Master, occasionally assisted by his father William Buzzard senior, the former master, who was born in 1726. Mr. James Buzzard was a somewhat severe, but so far as his attainments went, a very good [10] teacher. One of the rules of the school was that the children might attend as long as they pleased before beginning to write, but at the expiration of three years from the time of their entering the writing class, whatever their age or wishes their attendance at the school must cease, so far as the endowment was concerned: those parents who sent their children longer being compelled to pay for their education. My father said he was desirous for me to learn all that the Master could teach me, and that therefore I should enter the writing-class in October 1805, and he would pay for me three or four years after the expiration of the endowment term. Such was my father's purpose, but God's purpose was widely different, and apparently far more adverse to my acquiring knowledge.

I could not form a letter when I entered the writing class, but could write figures long before. I well remember when I was less than four years old my father [11] held me up in his arms and taught me the figures from the face of our house clock. He also taught me to extract the square root, some of the simpler problems of which I recollect to have correctly solved before I was six years old, *i.e.* before I could form a letter, or part of a letter.

Though I have written several myriads of pages, writing has always been a bore to me. When at school I never liked writing, and consequently did not learn to write well: but in spelling, reading and ciphering I presently stood first in the school. But alas! in the month in which I completed my eighth year I, in common with my father and mother and nearly all the family were stricken down by fever. Its attack on me was but slight, and all the others, save one, were mercifully spared: but the unspared victim was my dear and honoured father, who after a few days of severe suffering and prostration sunk beneath the [12] malady on June 23rd 1807, aged 32 years. His assets being insufficient to pay his debts, his stock in trade and household furniture were sold by auction. This was done not merely with the consent of my beloved mother, but the proposal was in my hearing made by her to the principal creditor. Circumstances shamefully unjust to all the creditors were connected with the sale, in circumstances which were specially cruel and vexing to my mother, who at no time in her protracted life, not even in the years of her deepest penury, ever contracted a debt which she did not promptly and honourably pay. On the very day of my father's interment, one of his brothers applied for letters of administration to his effects. Those being obtained a few days subsequently, he thereupon forthwith brought the auctioneer, who having concluded the sale and received its proceeds said, "Had we not better place this money in Kettering Bank until you settle with the creditors?" [13] "Oh no!" said my uncle, "I will take care of it." How far he took care of it I know not: but I do know that none of the creditors ever received a penny of it!! And not only so, but my dear mother travelled many scores of miles in collecting debts owing to my father, and forthwith paid the proceeds to my uncle under whose instructions she had collected them, not a penny of which ever found its way to the creditors!!! I have since found reason to believe that my uncle was himself hopelessly insolvent, and that his own sale was staved off by the money of which he defrauded my father's creditors. I suppose their knowledge of this prevented them from taking the legal measures against him which they might have done.

By the death of my father my mother was in the thirty second year of her life suddenly plunged into the very depths of poverty. She felt this keenly, very keenly, and shed many, very many, bitter tears over her bereavement [14] and its painful consequences: but her faith in the God of the widow and the fatherless did not fail. And her faith was honoured, though not so as to preclude our undergoing some severe privations. Several of the rate-payers were persons of great wealth, and a large part of the land in the lordship is some of the best pasturage in England, yet the parochial allowance doled out to the widow and four young children of an industrious tradesman was seven shillings a week, almost all the necessaries of life being at that time fully double, and some of the principal much more than double their present price! My sister, however, having been brought up my our grandfather, Ayer, the Baptist Minister at Braybrook, she, of course, continued chiefly to reside there: but the parish officers having on that account cruelly deducted a shilling and sixpence a week from their scanty dole, she came to reside with us for a time, which compelled them to [15] raise our allowance to its former amount.

I continued to attend the Free School for a year after my father's death. At the end of June 1808 I visited my father's and mother's relatives at Kettering, staying with them six weeks, in which time I saw the presentation of the splendid sword presented by the Kettering Volunteers in July of that year to their commander J. C. Gotch, Esq.[11] Scarcely had I returned to Hallaton ere I was employed in scaring birds from a field of wheat, for which I received the magnificent payment of twopence a day: but this being the first money I ever earned has always stood out distinctly and pleasingly on my Memory's Tablet.

In October 1808 Mr. Buzzard informed me that my three year's membership of his writing class had expired. My mother being too poor to pay for my further teaching I was compelled to leave school. Thus when a little more than nine years old my education terminated, [16] save that I subsequently gathered a small amount of additional knowledge in the Sunday School. During the few months in which I continued to live in Hallaton Mr. Buzzard taught me more of arithmetic, a service which however kindly soever intended, I have for half a century deemed a desecration of the Sabbath.

My father's youngest brother, a journeyman shoemaker, resided at Tilton, a village about six miles from Hallaton, being an excellent penman, the clergyman of that parish offered him the mastership of the Charity School, but as he had very little knowledge of arithmetic he requested my mother to allow me to reside with him for a time, to which she reluctantly consented. I consequently went to live at Tilton in February 1809, and thus became at nine years and eight months old a schoolmaster's teacher and virtual governor of the school, my uncle being almost wholly away at his employment in a shoemaker's [17] shop in another part of the village. On Sundays he, of course, officiated in the school. I believe all the parents of the children were satisfied with the progress they made.

I left on Good Friday, and came with my mother to spend Easter with our relatives at Kettering, not knowing the things which she had arranged to befall me there. Mr. Waters, whose second wife was my

11 John Cooper Gotch (1772-1852) was proprietor of Kettering's Bank and also of the only wholesale footwear business in the town. A Baptist, he was a Deacon and a leading figure at Little Meeting. In the wars against the French he patriotically raised and paid for a troop of Volunteers in Kettering for civil defence.

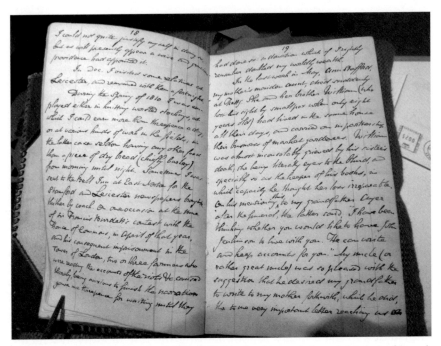

Figure 2. Pages 18 and 19 of "My Life" in Jenkinson's hand. (*Ann Jenkinson*)

aunt, was a tailor and draper in High Street, Kettering. My mother had requested him to take me on trial with a view to an apprenticeship. Both he and my aunt were so kind to me that I believe my indenture would have been prepared and signed in the course of a year, but his three sons by his first wife treated me so unfairly that I refused to stay. I therefore left in October, the knowledge I had acquired during the six months in the use of thimble, needle and thread being such as to be of some service to me in my pilgrimage of life. My mother blamed me for leaving, and [18] I could not quite justify myself in doing so but, as will presently appear, a wise and gracious providence had appointed it.

In December I visited some relatives at Leicester, and remained with them a fortnight. During the Spring of 1810 I was employed either in knitting worsted stockings, at which I could earn more than three pence a day, or at various kinds of work in the fields, in the latter case seldom having any other food than a piece of dry bread (chiefly barley) from morning until night. Sometimes I was sent to the *Bell Inn* at East Norton for the Stamford and Leicester newspapers brought thither by coach. On one occasion, at the time of Sir Francis Burdett's contest with the House of Commons,[12] in April of that year, and his consequent

---

12 Burdett was a patrician Radical who won a famous election in Westminster in 1807. When he protested against the House of Commons committing a man to prison illegally, he in

imprisonment in the Tower of London, two or three farmers who were reading the accounts of the riots etc. caused thereby, being anxious to finish the narration, gave me three pence for waiting until they [19] had done so: a donation which, if I fully remember, doubled my worldly wealth.

[John and Edward Jenkinson find work in Kettering]

In the last week in May, Ann Stafford, my mother's maiden aunt, died suddenly at Kettering. She and her brother William (who lost his sight by smallpox when only eight years old) had lived in the same house all their days, and carried on in partnership their business of market gardeners. William was almost inconsolably grieved by his sister's death, she being literally eyes to the blind, and specially so as the keeper of his books, in which capacity he thought her loss irreparable. On his mentioning this to my grandfather Ayer after the funeral, the latter said, "I have been thinking whether you would like to have John Jenkinson to live with you. He can write and keep accounts for you." My uncle (or rather great uncle) was so pleased with the suggestion that he desired my grandfather to write to my mother forthwith, which he did, the, to me, very important letter reaching us [20] on the morning of Hallaton Fair day, and my mother and I, presently deciding that I should accept the offer, arrangements were made with a travelling draper of Rothwell, who had a stall at Hallaton fair, that he should bring me to Rothwell on the Saturday, which town we reached in the afternoon of that day, and I was there hoisted to the top of Mr. Toon's wagon load of coals, thus returning to Kettering on June 2nd, 1810: a day always to be remembered by me as that on which I entered the groove of temporal prosperity, and also as that on which I became an inmate of the house which was to be my home for more than thirty three years, my central home in all the other years of my life's pilgrimage, the home on part of the premises of which I still reside, and in which I hope to die.

The purpose of Providence in having prevented me from consenting to become a tailor began now to be developed. I presently began to be fond of gardening, and to like my master (whom I generally called uncle), [21] and he in return was fond of me. After having lived with him nearly two years, he and I started from Kettering early in the morning of April 28th, 1812, on our journey to Market Harborough, in the Town Hall of which town I was bound to him as a "Parish Apprentice."[13] We returned to Kettering in the afternoon of the same

turn was arrested and imprisoned illegally. This led to huge protests in London and he was released. At the time of the wars against Napoleon and fears of "Jacobinism", there was severe governmental repression of free speech.

13 His native parish of Hallaton paid the premium for his apprenticeship.

Figure 3. The Rev. Andrew Fuller, Minister of Little Meeting Baptist chapel, (1782-1815), a major influence on the young Jenkinson.
(*Author's collection*)

day. I never knew anything experimentally of the hardships endured by not a few parish apprentices. My master always treated me with unfailing kindness, and I in return served him industriously and faithfully, frequently, even when quite a lad, keeping pace with the men with whom I had to work, and from February to October in each year working every day more hours than they.

Having, when living with my uncle Waters in 1809, been appointed a monitor in Mr. Fuller's Sunday School, I was reappointed on my return to Kettering in 1810: but not liking some things in the school, I left it after a few months. Nevertheless, I continued regularly to attend the chapel, and in the course of the five years [22] immediately preceding his widely lamented death I heard Mr. Fuller expound the whole of the Acts, the Epistle to the Romans, and part of the first Epistle to the Corinthians: his unequalled expository labours being terminated by his decease when he had reached the middle of the fourth chapter of the past-named epistle.

I shall never forget some of the weighty sentences which fell from his lips. Take for instance on Romans 9.16 "So then it is not of him that willeth, nor of him that runneth, but of God that sheweth mercy." "It *is* him that willeth and him that runneth,"said he, "who escapes hell and reaches heaven: But it is not *of* him. The salvation of a sinner is found *by* him who seeks it, yet it is not *of* him, but of God which sheweth mercy."

I heard him preach his last sermon on April 2nd, 1815, from Isaiah 66.2. Its three leading ideas were God's approval of poverty of spirit, or genuine humility: of contrition of spirit, or true repentance: of tenderness of spirit, or a godly shrinking from sin and temptation.

[23] My usual seat in the chapel being next to the wall of his house, I was within a few feet of him when he entered into rest while his assistant, the Rev. J. K. Hall, was preaching on Lord's day morning May 7th, 1815 and heard the very appropriate sermon which Mr. Hall preached in the afternoon of that day from Isaiah 9.mid-6 "The government shall be upon *his* shoulders." At the funeral on May 15th, I stood close to the coffin during the whole service, and therefore, of course, heard Dr. Ryland preach the funeral service from Romans 8.10.

On September 11th 1814 I went to Boughton House to see the Duchess of Buccleuch (the mother of the present Duke) lie in state, and walked from thence by the side of the funeral procession to be a spectator of her funeral in Warkton Church, and amongst the mourners well remember seeing the Earl of Chatham (eldest son of the great Earl Chatham, and brother of the celebrated William Pitt) and also Lord Sidney, both of whom I believe near relatives of her Grace. The funeral taking place on the Lord's day, my being present on the occasion was [24] such an inroad on my habitual attendance at public worship that although I reached Kettering in time for the afternoon and evening services, my conscience was disturbed by my desecration of the Sabbath. Nevertheless about fourteen months subsequently I was guilty of a more flagrant deviation from my customary course. On Sunday, November 12th, 1815, the inhabitants of Kettering were extensively drawn aside from their propriety by the information that the Prince Regent (afterwards George the Fourth) would pass through our town on his way from Leicestershire to dine with the Earl of Westmoreland at Apethorpe, and that he would probably arrive at Kettering shortly after two o'clock. In common with very many others, I was thereby led to absent myself from the house of God. H.R.H. did not arrive until between five and six o'clock, and it being then dark, and the windows of the royal carriage being closed, not more than one person in five hundred of those who had gathered to see him obtained even a glimpse of his hat. At six o'clock I went to chapel, and heard our [25] minister, the Rev. J. K. Hall, preach an unusually powerful and convincing sermon "On the sanctification of the Sabbath required of us" (Text, Genesis 2.3). He had delivered the same sermon about two years previously, but its influence on my mind was immeasurably greater on its repetition than when I first listened to it: a fact easily accounted for by the accusations of my conscience on the later occasion: though sad to say the impressions then produced were too speedily obliterated.

By a remarkable coincidence this was on the first Lord's day after Mr. Hall's ordination as Mr. Fuller's successor in the pastorate of the Baptist Church at Kettering. The very powerful sermon above referred to was probably a divine answer to the many fervent petitions offered for him and by him in connexion with his ordination. I was told that the Rev. T. N. Toller[14] preached on the same subject in his chapel on the following Sunday morning, and that in the course of his sermon he said, "If His Royal Highness were [26] now present I would tell him that he had not only himself desecrated the Sabbath, but also thereby set a baleful example to the nation at the head of which the King of Kings had placed him."

I vividly recollect the very large and splendid comet which passed near to the North Pole in September 1811, and heard the striking sermon in reference thereto preached on a Sunday morning in that month by the Rev. T. N. Toller from Psalms 95.8. I also heard the sermon he preached on a Wednesday evening in September 1820 in reference to the large eclipse of the sun on the seventh of that month. On the next day I wrote down as much of the sermon as I could remember. This manuscript will be found amongst my papers. Text, Joel 3.15 "The sun and moon shall be darkened, and the stars shall withhold their shining."

I was an early depositor in the Kettering branch of the Northampton Savings Bank. The excellent Henry Lamb, Esq.[15] being appointed as Receiver of deposits at Kettering. I called at [27] his office to make a deposit of twelve shillings. He expressed his pleasure that I had come. He said the Savings Bank is intended for just such youths as you. On reaching home, and reading the Rules I learnt that no lesser sum than twelve and sixpence would acquire interest, I therefore in the course of a short time made a further deposit of three shillings. At that

---

14 Thomas Northcote Toller was minister of the Independent chapel, Great Meeting, from 1775 to 1821. In turn, he was succeeded by his son, Thomas (1796-1885). In 1875 the church celebrated a hundred years of a consecutive Toller father-and-son ministration. Thomas Toller retired shortly after, completing a ministry of fifty-five years. Thereafter the church became known as Toller Congregational.

15 Henry Lamb (1791-1862), solicitor, was the founder of the legal firm of Lamb & Stringer. It was at this time that a Savings Banks Act was passed to provide banking facilities for small savers.

time all moneys deposited in Savings Banks were not merely invested in Government Securities, but in the actual purchase of stock in the National Funds, so that on the withdrawal of deposits the amount received was not only that deposited with interest added thereto, but was greater or less according as the National Stocks had risen or fallen. This caused additional trouble to the Savings Bank officials, and had the price of stocks declined would doubtless have excited dissatisfaction in the minds of depositors. The government therefore wisely decided that no future deposits should be affected by the rise or fall of the national funds. These having [28] steadily [risen] during the not very long time my few shillings had been deposited, the addition thereto was, if I rightly remember, more than ten *per cent*.

Though generally spending my winter evenings in the pursuit of knowledge I, from infancy, occasionally mingled with my companions in their sports and pastimes, and therefore sometimes had the subsequently great William Knibb[16] as a playmate. But in the first week of November 1818, when, though short in stature and boyish in appearance, I was old enough to have known and done better, I got myself into temporary difficulty, and as some thought, disgrace. It had, for many years, been customary to kindle a bonfire on the fifth of November on Kettering Market Hill. But in that year a tradesman in the town who was inflated in a large amount of self-consequence, and whose political views were antagonistic to those of many of his neighbours, finding himself newly-invested with a little brief authority as constable of the parish resolved that no bonfire should be lighted. Of course, he succeeded in his purpose: but not [29] until after there had [been] two or three minutes of scuffling. It that scuffle I took no part, but stood with both my hands in my pockets. The constable, however, having heard me say "When the proud are in office, the poor are trampled underfoot," I, with eight or nine others older than myself, was summoned before the magistrate. The evidence against us was, in part at least, exaggerated and untrue. The result was that we were bound to keep the peace for twelve months: the said "peace" not one of us having any intention or desire to disturb. The sympathy of our fellow townsmen in general was strongly in our favour.

[*Jenkinson inherits his master's business*]

On the 10th of May 1819 death deprived me of my beloved uncle and master, in the sixty-third year of his age. This was the first

16 William Knibb (1803-45) a Kettering Baptist missionary to Jamaica became a Nonconformist hero in the 19th century. Just after Christmas 1831, believing that the slave owners were delaying emancipation, a slave revolt broke out which was savagely repressed. Knibb took the slaves' side and came to England to speak for them. For this he was bitterly attacked by the plantation owners and their friends. His name is still revered in Jamaica.

personally afflictive bereavement I had sustained: for, though I felt a childish sorrow when my father died, I was not then old enough to appreciate the magnitude of that loss. But my dear master was in many [30] ways a second father to me. During nearly nine years that I served him he never, that I recollect, spoke to me an angry word, though assuredly he spoke to me thousands, yea myriads, of words of kindness and encouragement. He was truly an extraordinary man. Deprived, as he was, of the pleasures and advantages of sight, he was rarely downcast, but habitually cheerful, and frequently facetious. He was a skilful musician, and in all sorts of weather the principal bass singer in the choir of the parish church. He had considerable knowledge of astronomy, and was the first who gave me any idea of that science. The rapidity and correctness with which he solved difficult problems by mental arithmetic often astonished me. His remembrance, especially of human voices, was amazingly retentive. Repeatedly, when accosted by a soldier who had been absent from the town seven, ten or even fifteen years, he would respond "Ah John, [31] or George, etc., how are you?" when those who could see failed to recognize their former neighbour. The fact, however, is that after attaining the age of about twenty years a man's voice undergoes a less amount of change than almost everything else pertaining to him. Different attire may render his recognition difficult, his hair may have become bleached by terror, by grief, by study, or by age, or his natural covering may have given place to an artificial one, time may have ploughed his furrows on the cheek, obesity may have been exchanged for leanness, or leanness for obesity, and the once erect and firmly knitted spine may have been compelled to bow itself, but amidst all these and other metamorphoses the voice remains to a great degree unchanged.

Though unable, even amid the light of noontide to discern a single step of his way my master never availed himself of the aid of a walking-stick, except when journeying from one town or village to another: yet he was [32] almost every day on foot for many hours either at work in his garden or carrying its produce from thence to his dwelling-house. Although knowledge was at one entrance "quite shut out", all his other senses were remarkably acute. Take one illustration out of many. Sixteen years before I was born, his father purchased a garden planted with fruit trees, etc. In June of that year my blind uncle and his sister Ann went into that garden to gather gooseberries, wishing especially to gather *green* ones, *i.e.* those which would continue to be green when ripe. Those on all the trees were, of course, all that time green, and neither brother or sister know from former experience which would not be so when ripe. Ann said, "William here is a beautiful green tree here." On reaching it he said, "These are *red* ones." "No," she replied, "I will lay you a wager of half an ounce of snuff that they are green ones." The wager was laid, and when the summer's sun had ripened [33] the fruit, the blind man won it. He told me he was sure he was right, because he felt that the hairs on the gooseberries of that tree were stiffer than those of green ones are. The retail price of snuff was then three halfpence per ounce, consequently the fruit of that tree and its off-shoots has from [that] time until now been called by us "the three farthing sort". I have personally gathered large quantities of fruit from that identical tree.

Greatly as I loved my master, and much as I have cause to remember him with gratitude, the thought of him is often insufferably painful to me. Oh, that I knew that he has entered into eternal blessedness! Oh, that I were half so sure that he loved Christ, as I am that he loved me! Had I an atom of faith in the efficacy of prayers for the dead, I would pray for him with unwearied importunity. But I know full well that that would be of no avail. I am not without a vestige of hope respecting him, but I desiderate a brighter hope. My [34] lack of this is part of the penalty I justly have to pay for not having myself become a Christian earlier. Had I done so, I must have told him, and as I know he would have allowed me to speak to him about his soul more directly and frequently than he would have liked from others, I might have been the means of his becoming a decided Christian too. May God forgive my procrastination, for I shall never forgive myself for it.

My master inherited his dwelling house and premises from his father, John Stafford (referred on pages 5 & 6), the garden, containing an acre of land (mentioned on page 32) being inherited by my master's elder brother, John Stafford the younger, who, being a dissipated man, presently sold it to his blind brother, who in completing the purchase had to obtain a mortgage upon it to the amount of sixty pounds. The house was free from encumbrance.

I can most truly aver that I never had a moment's thought or expectation that they [35] would ever become mine, except that perhaps I might succeed in purchasing them. I had once heard my master incidentally say to a friend that he had by his Will (made many years before I came to live with him) directed all his property to be sold, and the proceeds thereof to be divided amongst his nearest relatives: a disposition which I was aware would give me no share of it whatever, inasmuch as my grand-mother (my master's eldest sister) and my mother were then living. I never either directly or indirectly said a word to my master on this subject. I could not bear to think of his being removed from me by death.

Whether under other circumstances that Will would have been

cancelled I know not: but about two years previous to his death my master had the vexation of learning that a nephew of his (son of another sister) whom I anticipated as likely to become the purchaser of his uncle's property, and his successor in the business, had commenced in opposition to him as nursery and seedsman. I believe that [36] from that time he had resolved to make another Will, but it was not actually made until about forty hours before his death. On the Will being read after the funeral I was astounded to find that he had bequeathed the whole of his property to me, on condition of my paying certain legacies to his relatives, and providing another of his sisters, who had for many years generally resided with us, with a maintenance for her life. The residue was not large, being scarcely more than £150, but it was worth four times that sum to me: and moreover gave me a start in life such as I never hoped to receive. It was also specially valuable to me as evidencing that my master knew that I had served him faithfully, and that he was fully satisfied with my services. It moreover presented a notable instance of providential retribution. I had, solely from regard to my master's interest, made many improvements in his garden, without any idea that they would benefit myself, but on the [37] contrary in the belief that by thus causing the garden to fetch a higher price, it would require me to borrow a larger sum should I become the purchaser. But now, in the unanticipated movements of divine providence, all these improvements were to my own decided advantage: while, on the other hand, the relative who, anticipating that I might grow up to become his rival, had prematurely commenced business in opposition to my master, had thereby taken the very step which facilitated what he was so anxious to prevent. As I then had a very juvenile appearance, he said I was not old enough to manage the business, and that I should very soon waste the property of which I had become the possessor. It is needless to add that neither part of this prediction was verified by fact.

Justice to the memory of the relative above referred to requires it to be stated that, though at that time he spoke hard things against me, we never, either then or at any [38] other time had a moment's altercation. It may also be added that, though he never had a month's schooling, he was a very clever and well-informed man, an acute and almost invincible disputant, an accurate land surveyor: and the delineator of our excellent map of Kettering as it existed nearly half a century ago.[17] He became a good man, was baptized by the Rev. J. K. Hall, and joined his church after I left it. And yet he, until his death, regularly paid for a sitting in my chapel, which he always attended on Sunday evenings, and never failed to contribute to the New year's gift with

17 This was Robert Smith, who published *A Plan of the Town of Kettering in the County of Northamptonshire. First delineated by Mr. Eagle, 1804, Corrected to the Present Time*, 1826.

which my friends presented me. He had a clear view of the way of salvation, died happy in Christ, and I have no doubt is now in heaven.

Immediately after the death of my master, my brother Edward came to reside with me, and for nearly nine years served me as honestly, and earnestly and as laboriously as I had for nearly nine years served my predecessor: thus verifying the scriptures adage, "With the same measure that [39] ye mete it shall be measured unto you again."

Although I had for nine years been the juvenile member of a family whose three seniors (my master, his sister, Mrs. Cave, and her daughter Hannah Cave) were regular attendants at the parish church, I was from the first allowed to attend the Baptist Chapel, which I regularly did, except that, on Sunday evenings when there was no preaching at chapel, I frequently went to church, and also occasionally on a Sunday morning in icy weather, when it was thought unsafe for my master to go unaccompanied.

[*Jenkinson's Baptist Conversion*]
At that time, as for many years previously, the Independent Chapel in Kettering (the Rev. Thomas Northcote Toller's) was almost invariably called "the *Great* Meeting", the Baptist Chapel (the Rev. Andrew Fuller's) the *Little* Meeting. I have already stated that I sat under Mr. Fuller until his death in 1815. I continued my attendance under his successor, the Rev. John Keen Hall (nephew of the great Robert Hall, and grandson of the elder Robert Hall, pastor of the Baptist Church [40] at Arnesby, and author of *Help to Zion's Travellers*). When young I was warmly attracted to Mr. J. K. Hall's ministry, and often fell deeply under his preaching. I was sometimes almost persuaded to become a Christian, but, my heart being still unrenewed, my impressions speedily wore off, and I continued to live without Christ, without good hope, and without God in the world. O, how great are my obligations to sovereign mercy that I was not left to live in this sad state until Death found me still unfit for heaven, and consequently swept me into the gulf of everlasting woe! But the wonder-working grace of God prevented this.

On Lord's day, May 13th, 1821, my honoured grandfather, the Rev. John Ayer, who had for nearly fifty years been an humble but useful Baptist Minister, entered his pulpit for the last time. In the morning and afternoon of that day he had preached at Langton, near Market Harborough, but when about to name his text in the same chapel in the evening he fell backward [41] in the pulpit, and though he survived until Tuesday, he never spoke again on earth. On that memorable Sabbath evening, and I believe in the very hour in which the summons reached him while engaged in his Heavenly Master's work, I was arrested by the mighty hand of grace, my eyes were opened, my heart was changed, and my soul was plucked as a brand from the burning! Had my grandfather specially prayed for me on that day? Did his heart pray for me after he had lost the power of articulating his requests? Perhaps so, but whether thus or not, assuredly he and my honoured grandmother, my beloved mother, and other pious relatives and friends had often earnestly prayed for my conversion, and in answer thereto the boon implored was granted.

On the evening of the above named day, a respectable aged inhabitant of Kettering (Mr. Thomas Lee, Sen., farmer & baker) was interred in the burial ground adjoining the Independent Chapel, which was nearly filled on the occasion. [42] I had for two or three months previously paid my addresses to a poor but very amiable and moral young person. At the close of the funeral service I stood near to the chapel door waiting for her. I presently saw her come out, and had she then seen me my life history would probably have been widely different from what I have actually experienced. But just as I was about to follow her, a young man who twelve years before had been a fellow scholar and fellow monitor with me in Mr. Fuller's Sunday school, but who, having served his apprenticeship at a distance from Kettering I had seldom seen for several years, asked me to take a walk with him. That walk was, under God, the saving of my soul. Blessed be the Lord for giving me such a precious friend as William Dyson, and for having in his kind and wise providence appointed that walk for us.

The united monthly missionary prayer meetings at Kettering were commenced in, I believe, the year 1820. One advantage resulting therefrom was that many persons who had never thought [43] of attending an ordinary prayer meeting began to attend these united meetings. Of these I was one. On Monday, May 7th, 1821, the meeting was held in the Wesleyan Chapel, to which I accordingly went, though without any true fear of God in my heart. Having throughout the day been hard at work in the open air, and not having tasted an atom of food after twelve o'clock, I in the course of the service felt an overpowering dizziness come over me, and, having in previous years occasionally fainted away, I felt as though syncope would certainly again occur. I therefore rose from my seat in the gallery, firmly grasped the tops of the pews and the handrail of the stairs, and thus, in God's good providence, safely reached the open air without actually fainting. Some weeks subsequent to May 13th, my friend Dyson told me that his principal reason for asking me to take a walk with him on that evening was that he might have an opportunity of asking whether I had recovered, and how I felt. He said that [44] sitting in the opposite gallery he saw how ill I looked, and regretted that no one near offered to lead me down the stairs.

At that period the knotty points of Calvinism and Arminianism were much more frequently discussed in the conversation of young persons than they are now. At least this was the case in Kettering. Consequently my friend Mr. Dyson had not walked far ere that topic came uppermost. On my saying that man is naturally unable to do any thing good in God's sight, he meekly and sweetly replied, "But I think it is at least our duty to seek." From that moment I for weeks cared little or nothing about Calvinism or Arminianism. The arrow had gone straight to my conscience, and stuck fast in my heart. I returned home, but scarcely to sleep. On the Monday, my convictions of sin and danger were stronger and deeper than on the previous evening. On Tuesday, still more so. On Wednesday morning, the sad tidings reached us that my grandfather had died at Langton on the previous day. Not having heard of his illness, I was shocked and grieved by this intelligence. This, by shewing the blessedness of being ready for death, still further strengthened the work of grace in my soul. My sins stood before me as numberless, great and aggravated. I felt that, without Christ, I must inevitably be lost. And yet I scarcely think I had then begun to believe on him. On the following morning, to my consternation and alarm my convictions had subsided, my concern about my soul was almost gone! I noticed this as I was walking along Kettering Street, and instantly thought, "Oh! Now I shall certainly be lost for ever! I shall never again feel such concern! Assuredly I shall never feel a deeper concern! And these emotions, like all my former ones are fast dying out! Oh! I shall inevitably be lost for ever!!" At that moment the expressive stanza of Dr. Watts came powerfully to my remembrance,

[46]   "A guilty, weak and helpless worm,
         On thy kind arms I fall,
         Be thou my strength and righteousness,
         My Jesus and my all."

I did not merely recollect these words, but personally, earnestly, yea almost in an agony of spirit, adopted them for myself. I felt myself *"guilty"* and needing Christ's *"righteousness"*, but I felt this less powerfully than the words *"a weak and helpless worm"*, and *"be thou my strength"*. I felt that I had not an atom of strength of my own to revive or perpetuate my convictions, or to avert the perdition of my soul, and that unless Christ became in every sense "My saviour and my all" I must inevitably perish. I was therefore constrained to commit myself into his hands *just as I was*. I have never since questioned that I, at that instant, reached the momentous turning point of my history. See John

1.12,13. The spot on which I thus began simply to trust in Christ, has *ever* [47] *since been sacred* to my remembrance.

How many things, some of them, at the time, seemingly insignificant, were links in the golden chain of God's providence in bringing about this, to me, all important event. The origination of the united monthly prayer-meetings, ~ my attendance on May 7th without staying to take food, ~ my consequent faintness, ~ my looking so unwell, ~ my friend Dyson's happening to sit in the gallery opposite to me, ~ his kind concern about my health, the non-turning of a head on leaving the Independent Chapel on May 13th, etc., etc., etc. all were combined by God's unerring wisdom, and rendered effectual that by his grace.

I forthwith began to attend all the prayer-meetings, and also the preaching on weekday evenings. I found the prayer-meetings at seven o'clock on Lord's day mornings very sweet and profitable. Before my eyes were opened, necessitated as I was to rise early on other mornings, I was accustomed through half the week to count [48] on the indulgence in bed which awaited me on Sunday mornings, and when as I was rising a little after eight I saw members of the Baptist church pass my window as they returned from the Lord's day morning prayer-meeting, I frequently thought, "if rising in time to attend those meetings is a necessary part of the Christian character, I shall never be a Christian: for I am sure I should not like to rise so early every Sunday morning." Yet so completely and quickly were my feelings on this subject changed, that when only a few days after his conversation with me, my friend asked whether there was "anything in the way of my attending the Sabbath morning prayer-meetings." I instantly rejoined, "Oh, no. I have indeed to serve my swine, but I can easily do that after breakfast." "Then call me at a quarter before seven next Sunday morning," said he. I did so, and throughout twenty five years, in summer and in winter, in sunshine and in darkness, on fine mornings and on wet ones, [49] neither he nor I, when at home and well, were never absent from those meetings often more than once or twice in a year.

Several of Mr. Hall's sermons in 1821, especially one from James 5.13 "Is any among you afflicted? Let him pray", aided the progress of the work of grace in my soul: though I derived greater benefit from some preached in that summer by the Rev. Thomas Toller, Junr. who was then officiating on probation as successor to his father in the pastorate of the Independent Church. One sermon preached by him specially helped me, and set my mind at liberty. Text Acts 5.31. "Him hath God exalted with his right hand to be a Prince and a Saviour, for to give repentance to Israel, and forgiveness of sins". My own minister used very often to say, "If you want to be saved, you must repent and come to Christ: that is the only way." This advice led me to the conclusion that I must not come to Christ until I had repented [50] of my sins. I therefore often and earnestly endeavoured to repent. The more I tried to make my heart soft, the harder it seemed to become. Mr. Thomas Toller, however, set me right on that point. He distinctly said, "It is of no use attempting to repent before you come to Christ. You must come to Christ *for* repentance. Our text unmistakably tells us that God has exalted Him for the purpose of giving repentance as well as forgiveness of sins."

Six or seven other young persons having then recently begun to seek salvation, our intercourse was frequent, pleasant and useful: in addition to which we had the great advantage of frequent interviews with several poor but eminently pious aged Christians, whose acquaintance with scripture and clear knowledge of the profound truths of Christianity were such as I have never subsequently met with anywhere else in persons in their position in society. They had evidently been instructed by "a master in [51] Israel". All of them had, in fact, become members of the church during Mr. Fuller's pastorate, and had not only sat under him, but had followed and appreciated the masculine train of thought which his sermons usually presented, and had keenly relished and thoroughly digested the strong meat with which he spread their table.

Having for fifty years past been somewhat frequently employed in writing for the press it might not have been uninteresting to have said on page 28 that my earliest contribution was inserted in the *Northampton Mercury* in March 1818. A query had a fortnight previously appeared in that paper asking "Why Easter Sunday was on March 22nd (the day of the full moon) instead of the 29th? The prayer book expressly says 'Easter day is *always* the first Sunday *after* the full moon which happens upon or next after the twenty-first day of March, and *if the full moon happens upon a Sunday, Easter day is the Sunday after.'*" [52] This query was answered on the following Saturday by a writer who signed himself *Petavius Junior*. He said "Easter does not follow the *real* full moon, but the *mean* full moon. The latter falling in that year on March 21st, Easter was properly kept on the 22nd." I thought this reply calculated to mislead, inasmuch as the phrase "mean full moon" is an astronomical one denoting the time of the full moon and deduced from the mean (or average) hourly motions of the sun and moon: *i.e.* that which would be the time of the actual full moon were the orbits of the earth and moon both perfectly circular, *which neither is.* I therefore wrote a short letter to that effect, and said "the full moon which Easter follows might more appropriately be called the ecclesiastical full moon: for the tables published under the auspices, and by the authority of the Church of Rome and subsequently adopted by all Protestant nations, were constructed on the principle not of giving the exact astronomical time, but a very near practical approximation thereto, [53] and that as those tables shew the Ecclesiastical Full Moon to be on March 21st, 1818, Easter was rightly kept on the 22nd. *Scaliger* and *Petavius*, though not exactly contemporaries, having taken different sides on subjects akin to that of this letter, I, to place myself on a par with my antagonist, adopted the signature of *"Scaliger Minor"*, few readers probably suspecting that the said *Scaliger Minor* was a poor lad who was then serving his time as a *parish apprentice.*

As I have no copy either of my own letter or the others, I have, of course, only given their purport.

I have also omitted to state that I attended the public services connected with the ordination of the Rev. J. K. Hall as pastor of the Baptist Church at Kettering on November 8th, 1815, and consequently heard the admirable and faithful charge addressed to him by his uncle the Rev. Robert Hall (of which charge more hereafter) and the sermon to the Church (founded on Philippians 1.27) by the [54] Rev. J. Jarman, of Nottingham.

The Rev. T. N. Toller was suddenly called to his rest on February 26th, 1821, aged 66, having held the pastorate of the Independent Church at Kettering forty-five years. The last two sermons I heard him preach were one to the aged on December 31st, 1820, Text, Psalms 71. 17,18, the other to the young on January 7th, 1821, Text, Mark 9.35. I was present at his interment on March the 8th, and of course heard the funeral oration by the Rev. B. L. Edwards, of Northampton, and the eloquent and impressive funeral sermon by the Rev. R. Hall. Text, Hebrews 13.7.

On the third of October following, the Rev. Thomas Toller was ordained as successor to his honoured father: the ordination prayer being offered by the Rev. J. Horsey, of Northampton, the charge given by the Rev. T. P. Bull of Newport Pagnell, from Mark 13.33, the sermon to the people being preached by the Rev. W. Scott of Rothwell, from Hebrews 13.17. The Rev. S. Hillyard of [blank] [55] preached in the evening from I Chronicles 29.5. I was present at all these services, and after the lapse of forty six years still retain somewhat of the impression they produced. I am happy and grateful to have to record that throughout this protracted space of time a kind Providence has prolonged the valuable life, and continued the useful labours of the then young pastor, and spared him to reach the borders of a good and vigorous old age.[11]

On March 7th, 1822, the balloting for filling up the vacancies in the Northamptonshire Militia[18] took place. Kettering was that year requested to send only two persons, and singularly enough, though hundreds in the town were liable to the drawn, the lot fell to me and my friend, William Dyson. A club for providing substitutes was established in the town, which, however, I hesitated to join, but within the last three minutes I sent my subscription of four shillings, and in a quarter of an hour [56] learnt that I had acted wisely in so doing. Mr. Dyson, being from home, had not joined the club. Thus, providing a substitute, and other expenses attendant thereon, cost him I believe about three pounds. Including my subscription fee, the whole cost to me was ten shillings.

About this time, or a little earlier, my dear brother Edward, with whom I always slept, said to me as we were laying ourselves down in bed one Saturday night, "I think I shall go with you to the prayer meeting tomorrow morning." I was glad at heart to hear him say this, but had some self-reproach that I had not asked him to do so. It was, however, an illustration of the power of *silent* influence. He said, "Ever since you began to attend the morning prayer meetings I have been miserable while lying in bed. I felt that I had a soul to be saved, as well as you and that therefore I ought to rise and go with you." This he did, not merely on one Sabbath [57] or for a short time, but always afterwards from that time until his death: *i.e.* through thirty six years and upwards, during the whole of which protracted period he was scarcely ever absent from any of the means of grace, except when either unwell or from home.

Of course I did not long attend the prayer meetings before the conductor requested me to engage in prayer. I refused the first invitation, but complied with the second: and was positively startled at the sound of my own voice in prayer. My thus engaging led to an important domestic change and improvement. The family of which I was an inmate, being attendants at the parish church, had laxer views of Sabbath obligations than are generally entertained by Nonconformists. Consequently, though we never gathered either fruit or vegetables on a Sunday, a somewhat large quantity of both had from time immemorial been sold on that day at our house. And as I was too young and [58] too timid to originate an alteration in this respect, it continued to be thus, even after I had become nominally the master: though I personally took little or no

18 The Militia was a force raised for the defence of the realm against invasion or rebellion. Each county had to contribute a quota of men between the ages of 19 and 45 liable for military service. The drawing up of the list was done parish by parish. The Militia continued in existence until 1908, when it was renamed and remodelled as the Territorial Force.

part in the sale. My great aunt, who managed our domestic affairs, though rigidly attached to the forms and ceremonies of the Church of England, was, I believe, on the whole a real Christian. Within three days after my engaging in prayer in the vestry, some one told her of it: and consequently on the next Sunday evening she said to me, "John you pray in the vestry, I should like you to pray at home tonight if you will." "No," I said, "I will never pray at home until you leave off selling things on Sundays." I believe this reply struck home to her conscience, for she answered. "Well, if you wish us to leave off, we will sell on next Sunday, and tell the customers that we shall be glad if they will in future come on the Saturday night as we do not intend to sell any more on Sundays." "Very well," I said, "then next [59] Sunday night I will commence family worship." Which I did.

It had for more than fifty years been a sort of article of faith in our family that if the fruit was not sold on Sundays a large quantity of it would perish for want of purchasers. This belief had kept the consciences of the senior members of the household quiet in the midst of their Sabbath desecration, and in this belief a relative who had lived in our house for several years and was a highly esteemed member of Mr. Fuller's church said to me in the week after our resolve, "They tell me you are going to leave off selling things on Sundays. I fear you will lose a large part of your gooseberries, for we always sold so many on Sundays." To this I replied, "Well, it is *not* right to keep on, it *is* right to leave off: so we will do it, and trust Providence in reference to the loss." And verily Providence honoured our trust. I believe it is [60] within the truth to say that in the days of our Sabbath desecration we sometimes had as much fruit perish *in one year* for want of customers, as *in all the forty five years* which have elapsed during our Sabbath observance. The reason being that we made greater and more effectual efforts to dispose of it during the weekdays than we had previously done. So true is it that "Godliness has the promise of the life that now is, as well as of that which is to come": a truth illustrated by a somewhat ludicrous, yet vexing, instructive and profitable incident which occurred in the following year, and which will show that I had small cause for pharasaical exultation on account of Sabbath observance.

As the cattle in the meadows adjoining our garden sometimes broke through the fences, and, if not driven out, did great damage, I and my brother generally walked down to the garden immediately after breakfast on Sunday morning, to see whether all was [61] right. Having done so on the last Sunday in August, we saw the plums lie thickly on the ground. It just then began to rain, and seemed likely to be a wet day. I therefore said to my brother, "These plums will be nearly all spoiled before tomorrow morning: let us pick them up, and lock them in the barn." Consequently we presently collected considerably more than a bushel, and locked them up. But alas! on reaching the barn early on Monday morning, we found that the lock had been broken, and not only the plums all stolen, but the nearly new baskets and scuttles in which we had placed them all gone too. "Well," I said "this has at any rate taught me a lesson. I will never again on any account do a minute's needless work on a Sunday. If we had let the plums lie the thieves would have picked them all up, and almost certainly would not have stolen our baskets and scuttles." I have ever since that time strictly adhered to this resolution. [62] Thus this incident was amongst the "all things which work together for good."

[1822: Jenkinson becomes a member at Little Meeting]

Having regularly assembled with the Lord's people for considerably more than a year, and been repeatedly requested by them to join the Church, I felt myself under an obligation to publicly profess my allegiance to Christ, and consequently was proposed as a candidate for baptism and church membership. But an apparently insuperable obstacle soon confronted me on my way. From time immemorial it had been the custom of the Baptist Church, as of many others to require every male candidate to give to the church an *oral* account of the steps by which he was led from darkness to light, and of the Lord's subsequent dealings with his soul: or, as this was technically termed, "to speak his experience". For a young and timid person wholly unaccustomed to public speaking to do this in the face of a large church meeting, was no easy task. At Kettering, [63] however, and perhaps elsewhere, it was rendered more formidable still by the meeting at which the candidate was required to speak being open to the admission of strangers. These meetings were frequently held, not in the vestry but in the chapel. I had myself been present on more than one occasion, and had then witnessed such painful exhibitions that I resolved never to submit to such an ordeal, which I regarded as dishonourable to the church requiring it, unfeeling towards the candidates, and wholly unscriptural in its requirement. One member of the Church after another attempted to overcome my scruples, but without effect. One said, "Our custom is unquestionably scriptural. Did not David say, 'Come and hear, all ye that fear God, and I will declare what he hath done for my soul?'" "Yes," I replied, "but you forget that David was then neither a young man, nor a candidate for church-fellowship, but an advanced saint of the Lord: and I [64] could gladly, and no doubt profitably sit to hear some of you tell us of the Lord's dealings with you in your forty years wilderness pilgrimage: but this you omit. And are you not setting yourselves up as wiser than Christ and his apostles? Before what Church meeting were the three thousand on the day of Pentecost required to speak prior to their baptism?"

Others said, "You would not find speaking to us in public so formidable a task as you imagine." I replied, "The difficulty of speaking before you is not the main ground of my objection. Perhaps I could speak if I were to try, but I take my stand on the ground that you have no scriptural authority to *compel* me to do so. If any candidate wishes to speak his experience, I would neither prevent *him*, nor blame *you* for allowing it: but I say you have no right to *demand* it."

At last, one of the most intelligent [65] and pious members of the church came to me with what he evidently thought an unanswerable argument. "You forget," he said, "that it is not an earthly society, but a church of Jesus Christ which requires you to speak your experience, and you know that David says, 'The secret of the Lord is with them that fear him, and he will shew *them* his covenant.'" I replied, "Why that argument is the very essence of popery. Do not think for yourself, nor act for yourself, believe all the Church bids you, and you will infallibly be right."

As I would not join the church unless this rule was relaxed, Mr. Hall very kindly and properly permitted me, and any other of the candidates who pleased, to give our experience in writing. Those who preferred to speak, of course, did so. I believe this has been the custom from that time to the present.

[66] The obstacle in my path being thus removed, I and eight others (of whom one was a candidate for membership with the Independent Church in Kettering) were baptized by the Rev. J. K. Hall on November 3rd 1822, a day beyond all comparison the happiest I have seen on earth. O, if those who feel that they ought to be baptized, but procrastinate it from their apprehension that that ordinance is a ponderous cross, would but stoop to take up that cross they would find it so covered with love and peace and blessedness, that they would presently rejoice with joy unspeakable and full of glory. At least such was my own experience, and has been that of myriads besides.

The high opinion I had formed of professing Christians while looking at them, as it were, through the window, was speedily lowered when I found myself a member of the church. The very first church meeting I attended after my baptism, and also the one [67] held on Christmas day were painful ones, on account of a charge of gross immorality brought against a leading and wealthy member of the church. The accusation was denied, and denied even upon affidavit before a magistrate: but the evidence was so clear and strong as to leave an impression on the minds of a large proportion of the members, that it could not be refuted. To escape from the exercise of church discipline the accused withdrew, for a time, from the church membership, but the stain on his character was not thereby obliterated. Further experience has taught me that cases like that are rare exceptions, and that notwithstanding their unquestionable failings and imperfections Christians are truly the excellent of the earth.

In October 1822, my honoured mother was united in marriage to Mr. Joseph Whiting, a widower with nine children: and as his home was in Kettering, she, of course, came to reside there too. I did not like the match, [68] but there was great truth and propriety in what was said to me by Mr. Hall and others, "You must not oppose it for she is just the woman who is wanted in that family." And truly she was. All the children respected and loved her, some of them very much so: and, moreover, as nearly all of them married when young, it seemed only a few years ere she and her husband were left as the sole inmates of their dwelling.

Until our mother's marriage I, and my brother, had always spoken of Hallaton as our home: but of course her leaving it terminated our application of that term to our native place. Although I have often preached at Hallaton, and enjoyed many pleasant visits to friends there, it in 1822 ceased to be home. My youngest brother, (Christopher, now my only surviving one) came to Kettering with our mother.

[A change in Jenkinson's theological position]
The year 1823 was to me a [69] memorable one, and, through the greater part of its course, a very happy one. My health was good, my business prosperous, my mind expanding, the means of grace, especially the prayer-meetings truly sweet, my intercourse with Christian friends, both old and young (several of the latter having recently commenced their heaven-ward pilgrimage) pleasant and profitable. The spring of that year was specially notable for the change in my theological views which then took place. Until that time I had been an Arminian: or rather without much knowledge or care for what name the learned might give it, the principal points in my system were

1. That God made man sinless, and without any tendency to sin. "Able to stand, yet free to fall."
2. That Adam in the exercise of his free agency disobeyed his maker's mandate, and thus "lost his garden and his God and ruined all his unborn race."
[70] 3. That thereby all mankind are so thoroughly undone as to be not only without righteousness, but also without power to do, or be, or desire anything spiritually good, But
4. That the Holy Spirit is given to every man in amply sufficient measure to enable him to repent and

believe, to pray and love, and to be holy in all
manner of conversation and godliness.

In my ignorance and short sightedness I imagined that these views
threw all the blame of the sinner's perdition on himself, and secured all
the glory of salvation to God, who had given such grace unto men.

One of the pious and intelligent individuals who had joined the
church during Mr. Fuller's pastorate was named Thomas Smith, who
subsequently married mother's sister. He was a silk weaver by trade,
and generally very poor in purse. He was a very nervous and somewhat
eccentric man, but eminently well-informed and judicious [71] on
religious questions. If through nearly half a century my religious views
have been in any measure accordant with scripture, I owe it under God
very much to my many conversations with that working-man. In fact,
he was to me what Joseph Diver was to Andrew Fuller in *his* early days.
The knotty points of Calvinism and Arminianism were often discussed
in conversation with my young associates, but with my seniors too, one
of the chief of the latter being Thomas Smith. On my stating to him the
four items of my creed above specified, he remarked, "The first three
points are scriptural enough, but I want an explanation of the last. You
say 'the Holy Spirit is given to every man'. Is it given to every man in
the same measure? If you say 'No, God does more for some men than
for others', that is Calvinism, or as I call it *Bibleism.*" "Oh no," I replied,
"I do not like attributing partiality or favouritism to God. He is the
Father of all, and no respecter [72] of persons, and therefore I believe he
gives to all *equally.*" To this he replied, "O then I see that when you get
to heaven, you will not have to thank God but *yourself* for getting there.
If God has done no more for you than for Judas, or for those who drop
into hell everyday, you must have made yourself to differ, and
consequently will for ever have cause to thank yourself. You *may* have
to thank God for sending Jesus Christ, but you will clearly not have to
thank him for his Holy Spirit, because if your views are right, many
who have that Spirit as much as you, perish eternally: and if he has done
no more for you than for them you would have perished too, had it not
been for your own wisdom, or goodness, or prayers, or endeavours, or
whatever else you please to call it."

This conversation, and others similar thereto, led me to suspect
that Arminianism was neither the scriptural not the rational system I
had believed it to be. This [73] suspicion was confirmed and carried into
full conviction by my reading and rereading Jonathan Edward's[19]

---

19 Jonathan Edwards was a New England minister who was one of the founders of the
   Evangelical Movement in the mid-18th century. Amongst the many he influenced were the
   Wesley brothers and Philip Doddridge.

masterly work on the *Human Will*, until I seemed to understand every point of his argument. The works of Andrew Fuller, especially in controversy with Dan Taylor, Elisha Coles *On Divine Sovereignty*, and other works on the same subject firmly established that conviction: yet I neither *then* nor at any other time, doubted the obligation of sinners to believe in Christ, nor that the perdition of the lost is caused solely, or at least mainly by themselves. In short, my theological views have from that time until now been substantially those of Mr. Fuller, whose name is ever fragrant to my remembrance.

This change of sentiment naturally rendered Mr. Hall's preaching less congenial to me than heretofore: but I never on that account absented myself from the Lord's house. Whosoever else was absent, my place in the [74] chapel, in the Sunday school (in which I had been a teacher four or five years), at the Lord's table, at the Sunday morning and Monday prayer meetings, and at Thursday evening preaching, was very rarely empty. How pressing soever might be the claims of business on weekday evenings, I and my brother Edward regularly postponed them to the higher claims of religion, and we frequently remarked to each other that we seemed to do quite as much work on those days as on any others: the cause of this being doubtless found in our diligent improvement of all the other hours of the day. I was also during the whole of 1823 a regular collector for the Baptist Missionary Society, to which office I was appointed by the church shortly after my baptism. But my services in these directions were destined presently to cease.

[*The secession from Little Meeting, 1824*]
In the summer of 1823 Mr. William James (who died in 1867 having for several years previous to his death been the honourable and useful [75] senior deacon of the church) was led by providence to remove his residence from Lubenham, near Market Harborough, to Kettering, where he had been baptized a few months before me. Although previously personally unknown to each other, he had scarcely pitched his tent in Kettering ere an intimacy sprang up betwixt us. In the spring of that year we had begun to hold prayer-meetings in different houses in the town on Lord's day evenings after the close of the services in the chapels in the town. These meetings were attended by a large number of young members and inquirers and were found to be very sweet and profitable. At these meetings Mr. James was a welcome addition to our number. On three or four of us conversing at his house respecting them he said, "We used at Harborough to speak from texts of scripture which we chose for each other. Could we not do the same at Kettering?" I little imagined the influence which this question would exert on my future destiny. The suggestion was listened

to and approved. [76] But I said, "I will not be the first to speak, neither should I like any other person to choose a text for me to speak from." In accordance with this reply, it was agreed that each select his own text: that the speaking should take place on the first Lord's day in each calendar month, and that Mr. John Eyet should speak on August 3rd, I on September 7th, and Mr. James on October 5th. Mr. Eyet spoke in Mr. James' house in Job's Yard, I in William Toseland's house in the same part of Kettering, and Mr. James in Mr. Hollidge's house in High Street.

The passage of scripture from which I spoke was Deuteronomy 32.10. "He found him in a desert land, and in the waste-howling wilderness, he led him about, he instructed him, he kept him as the apple of his eye." Hundreds of times since that day it has seemed to me very remarkable that I should have selected *that* text. I had neither heard it preached from any one, nor read a sermon, [77] essay, tract or comment upon it: indeed I was then without a commentary of any kind. The text appears so unlikely to be chosen by a *young* man that I have little doubt that the Spirit of God was the principal agent in the choice, as foreshadowing my future history and experience. At any rate it is singularly descriptive of my life and history. I that evening said many things which I then *believed* to be true, but which I now *know* to be so. The God of grace not only found *me* in a desert land and a waste-howling wilderness, but he has also led me about and "by a way which I knew not". He has, moreover, instructed me in the knowledge of myself, in the knowledge of the professing church, and in the knowledge of the world, and the vanity of its pursuits, in the knowledge of Christ, and in the knowledge of his word, and especially in the knowledge of himself, his faithfulness and truth, his wisdom and his power, his mercy and his grace, and of his unfailing and unchanging love, [78] for He has indeed "led me about and still kept me as the apple of His eye".

From this it will be seen that September 7th, 1823, was a day which stands forth prominently among the days of my life. Though most of my hearers on that evening were young, there were among them some of riper years. One of the latter, who had been baptized by Mr. Fuller many years previously, was a poor, intelligent, but not perfectly sane old man. He said to me a few days subsequently, "If you mean to serve Christ zealously you will find two worlds against you." "How so?" I asked. He replied, "You will have the profane world and the professing world both against you." I rejoined, "I expect to have the profane world opposed to me, but surely you do not mean to say that professors of religion will oppose a person for serving Christ." "You will see, you will see," was his response. I do not believe he had an atom of external reason [79] for this response. I believe his remark to be one of those utterances which have a higher origin that human sagacity. And assuredly I presently did *"see"*. I had no imagination of any part of "the professing world" from which hostility to me was likely to arrive, neither I believe had he, but the good old man's prediction or anticipation was ere long verified by fact.

So large a number of persons attended these meetings, and the prayer-meetings we held on the intervening Sabbaths, that I was urgently requested to speak to them again, which I engaged to do at Mr. Waters' in High Street: but ere the arrival of the appointed day, (October 12th) our pastor, having heard of our meetings, determined to suppress them: a step which has ever seemed to me utterly uncalled for and unwise. We never held a meeting at the time there was either preaching or prayer at our own chapel or Mr. Toller's, and ourselves and all who assembled [80] with us were amongst the most regular attendants of all the services of the sanctuary. And so far from desiring to originate an opposition either to the church or its pastor, I can truly say I had no more thought of it than I had of asking to be appointed Commander in Chief of the British Army. Had we been left unmolested the zeal which was not amply supplied with oil would have burnt itself out, whilst that which was in association with perseverance would have sought another and a wider sphere. Moreover, had we been left alone, at the least twenty persons would in all likelihood have been soon added to the church as a result of these meetings.

But we were *not* left unmolested. Not merely was I censured from having spoken in the town, but also for having preached elsewhere!!! On September 14th, I had preached at Isham, and being strongly entreated to repeat any visit I promised to do so on October 12th. But Mr. [81] Hall told me I had no right to do so without having first obtained the sanction of the church of which I was a member!! I modestly asked, "Does church membership abrogate our civil and religious liberties? If a member of a church has an opportunity of speaking to a wicked man about his soul and salvation, is it requisite that he should obtain the sanction of the church before doing it? They that were scattered abroad in the persecution which arose about Stephen went everywhere preaching the word, and the hand of the Lord was with them, but we do not read of their either obtaining or asking for the sanction of the church before they did so." I said, moreover, that I was nevertheless quite willing to preach before the church if he wished it, but that I could not see that the church had any authority to compel me to do it.

I suspect that some of my friends had injudiciously extolled my preaching (if preaching it would properly be called), and that [82] this coming to Mr. Hall's ears stirred up his spirit against me. But, however this might be, it is certain that our meetings were bitterly denounced. Had we been kindly *requested* to discontinue them I believe we should at once have done so. But in this case, as in many others *"You shall not"*, was the parent of *"I will"*. At any rate I was not formed of the stuff which succumbs to threats and coercion.

Having continued occasionally to speak both in the town, and in some of the neighbouring villages until the first week in December, it was at the church meeting held in that week resolved that I should preach before the Church on Thursday December 11th, and also in the afternoon of Christmas day. On the first-named day I spoke from Psalms 136.23. "Who remembered us in our low estate, for his mercy endureth for ever": On Christmas day from Matthew 1.21, "Thou shalt call his name Jesus: for he shall save his people from their sins." [83] After my sermon on the last named day, the church unanimously awarded its sanction to my preaching, but expressed its wish that I should not again preach in Kettering, a wish which I religiously regarded so long as I remained a member of the church.

I may hereafter have occasion to specify several incidents which at the time of their occurrence seemed to be of trivial importance, but which in their issues proved to be the pivots on which the wheel of my life was turned. One incident of this kind may here find its appropriate place. In the middle of a market day in January 1824, one of our pastor's leading friends called on me to say that the Baptist Church at Aldwinkle wanted a supply for the next Sabbath, and to inquire whether I would go thither. Having at that time never been inside a pulpit, nor preached to a regular congregation I hesitated to return an answer: but at last [84] said, "I will ask Mr. Hall's advice respecting it, and let you know in half an hour." To this he assented, and I forthwith went to Mr. Hall's. On my, through his servant, requesting to see him for one or two minutes, she presently returned with the reply, "Mr. Hall is engaged: and therefore cannot see you." Influenced solely by diffidence and a fear of doing wrong I declined to supply at Aldwinkle on that occasion.

When I was at Mr. Hall's door a horse and gig stood before it, which I two or three days afterwards ascertained to belong to the gentleman who wanted me to officiate in his village chapel, and that Mr. Hall had thereupon sent his friend to me. Had Mr. Hall granted me a minute's audience, which I think he should have done, I believe he would have advised me to go, and in all likelihood that would have been the first step towards another sphere of labour than the one I occupied for twenty five years: [85] for assuredly I had neither the intention nor the desire to originate a second Baptist Church in Kettering, though some of my friends had already repeatedly urged it upon me, and subsequently took steps which presently brought it to pass.

I had prepared a minute account of the events which led to my secession from the Church of which I was a member: but as I have no wish to expose the failings of Christians who have long ago entered into heaven, nor to cherish the remembrance of wrongs which I have long ago forgiven, I gladly leave these things in the oblivion into which they sank. Suffice it to say that on Tuesday, February 10th, 1824, fifteen of us withdrew from the Church: a step which was not taken without much serious thought and earnest prayer. We held a very solemn and fervent prayer meeting on that evening, a meeting which, without our speaking of it as such, was a *real* ordination service, presided [86] over and sanctioned by the Head of the Church himself, and therefore leaving a lasting blessing behind it.

Yet the remainder of that week was one of the most solemn and distressing I have ever experienced. Like Guttenberg, the first printer, in the monastery of Abersgot, I seemed to hear two voices address me, the one bidding me to desist, the other to go forward nothing doubting. I felt sure that our withdrawment was, under the circumstances, necessary and right, and that had I been any one of my fourteen co-secessionists I should have heartily rejoiced in the decision we had adopted: but the thought of having to become the pastor of the little flock, and to have the care of souls, every one of which is a probationer for eternity brought with it an overwhelming sense of responsibility which well nigh crushed me. Having engaged to preach at Loddington on one of the evenings of that week I spoke from [87] Psalm LV. 22. "Cast thy burden upon the Lord, and He shall sustain thee, He shall never suffer the righteous to be moved." The counsel and the comfort of which text I was enabled to appropriate to myself, and found then, as I have habitually found in subsequent seasons, that the Gracious Master I served is truly a soul-sustaining and soul-preserving God.

I can with strictest truthfulness aver that I never in my life, either directly or indirectly, asked any individual to withdraw from Mr. Hall's church, or from any other, and to unite with us. My honoured and beloved mother regularly subscribed towards defraying the expenses of our chapel, but she lived and died a member of the church from which we had withdrawn. My dear brother Edward, who always felt a pleasure in doing anything and everything I wished him, remained behind for some time, and at last when he sent in his letter [88] of withdrawment, it was wholly without any advice or instigation from me. From the commencement of my ministry until now my aim has uniformly been to be the means of converting sinners to Christ, not to convert saints from one church to another. Consequently though several other members in addition to the first fifteen withdrew from Mr. Hall's church and joined themselves to us, it was certainly, so far as I was concerned, their own voluntary act.

[*Pastor of Ebenezer*]

Our first place of worship was the house opposite the *Sun* Inn, in Parkstile Lane, now Market Street. I went to it on the first Lord's day morning with somewhat of heaviness of heart, but the numbers present being far greater than my anticipation and the Lord's presence being sensibly vouchsafed us, I lost my burden, and went on my way rejoicing. I did not preach, as we had resolved to devote that day specially to prayer for the Lord's Blessing on our undertaking. [89] On the following Sunday morning (February 22nd) I preached from Psalm 90.16,17. "Let thy work appear unto thy servants, and thy glory unto their children. And let the beauty of the Lord our God be upon us: and establish thou the work of our hands upon us: yea the work of our hands establish thou it." In the evening from Romans 1.16. "For I am not ashamed of the gospel of Christ: for it is the power of God unto salvation to every one that believeth: to the Jew first, and also to the Greek." On the first Sunday in March I supplied the Baptist Church at Great Gidding, Huntingdonshire, and subsequently then for the first time entered a pulpit.

Our place of worship continued to be full every Lord's day morning, and densely crowded in the evening. We were therefore constrained to consider the propriety of erecting a chapel. For this purpose we purchased a farm belonging to Mr. George Warner, a member of the Society of Friends, and forthwith entered [90] into contract with carpenters, masons, etc. etc. Our pecuniary resources were extremely limited, but I felt certain that we had the approval of God, and that His resources being inexhaustible He would provide us with the means of defraying the cost; a faith which in our subsequent history was signally, indeed almost miraculously honoured. In conversing with my brother, before I had withdrawn from Mr. Hall's church I said, "It is of no avail our thinking of leaving, unless we are certain we can raise at least twenty pounds a year." "Twenty pounds a year," he replied, "Why, where in the world is it to come from?" And in March 1824 when the erection of a chapel was discussed at our church-meeting, some of the members said, "A new chapel is very desirable, but how shall we find the money to pay for it?" To which I responded, "Have we acted right in leaving Mr. Hall's Church? If we have *not*, let us all return to it again as soon as possible. If we *have* done right, [91] then God is with us, and will continue to be with us, and sooner than allow His cause amongst us to stand still for want of money He will transform the forms on which you are sitting into doubloons." In after years some of my friends sometimes playfully said to me, "The forms are not transformed into doubloons yet," to which my reply was, "Because that miracle has not yet been needed."

I laid the foundation stone of our chapel on Wednesday, May 26th, 1824, and preached in the evening of that day from Isaiah 28.16. "Therefore thus sayeth the Lord God, Behold I lay in Zion for a foundation a stone, a tried stone, a precious corner-stone, a sure foundation: he that believeth shall not make haste."

The chapel was opened for divine worship on July the 29th of that year. Being disappointed of the services of one of the preachers to whom we had applied, I preached the first sermon from Zech. 6.13. "He shall build the temple [92] of the Lord, and he shall bear the glory," and my highly-esteemed friend the Rev. Thomas Allen, pastor of the Baptist church at Irthlingborough, preached the second sermon. Text, Zechariah, 4.6,7. The day was a very pleasant and profitable one.

On the following Sunday morning I preached from I Kings 8. 57,58. "The Lord our God be with us, as he was with our fathers, let him not leave us, nor forsake us: that he may incline our hearts unto him, to walk in all his ways, and to keep his commandments, and his statutes and his judgements, which he commanded our fathers." In the evening, from II Chronicles, 6.18. "But will God in very deed dwell with men on the earth? Behold, heaven and the heaven of heavens cannot contain thee: how much less this house which I have built!"

I very frequently walked to Isham directly after dinner, preached there in the afternoon and returned to Kettering in time for the evening [93] service. On the Sabbaths on which I did not go we occasionally had as many as forty persons from Isham at our service at Kettering. One of the most intelligent and pious of them said to me, "My heart overflows with joy and gratitude. I have for years conducted divine service in my house at Isham. Have read the hymns, sang, read a sermon, and closed with prayer, without anyone except myself, either male or female, opening their lips, even to join in the singing: and now today I counted forty of my neighbours who were coming along the road from our village to your chapel."

I also frequently preached at Cransley, Broughton and other villages. When at supper on our chapel opening day, Mr. Allen said to me, "Now young man if you wish to fill your cage you must go out and beat the hedges." A hint on which I have extensively acted, without fee or reward, through a long succession of years, and not without abundant evidence of the Lord's blessing [94] attending my endeavours.

On the third Sunday in October 1824 I administered the ordinance of Baptism for the first time: Mr. Wilmot, now and for many years past, a leading member of Mr. Mursell's church,[20] being one of the four candidates, another of them, now nearly ninety years old, has for many years past resided, and still resides, in the white cottage at Olney which is given in the back-ground of the views of Cowper's house and Olney Church and parsonage in the illustrated edition of Cowper's poems.

Although our chapel was generally very well attended, and was sometimes quite filled, my regular congregation never was a large one. Indeed, the anticipation of my friend Thomas Smith (my Joseph Diver) though not literally verified by fact, was not very remote therefrom. Previous to the erection of the chapel he said to me, "I do not expect that you will gather a large number of persons to hear you regularly, but you will [95] do better than that, for I believe that all who *do* hear you regularly will become true Christians through your instrumentality." The accessions to our numbers were not great, but steady and encouraging. In addition to the four candidates just referred to, eight were baptized in 1825, six in 1826, five in 1827, five in 1828, and thirteen in 1829. Indeed during the quarter of a century of my pastorate at Kettering only two years elapsed without our receiving an increase. On one day in April 1841 thirteen were added to our number. Of course some chaff was found amongst the wheat, but certainly not more than the average experience of Christian churches in that respect. We were, moreover, favoured to enjoy not entirely uninterrupted harmony, but a measure of concord and Christian love beyond what churches in general are privileged to attain.

At our annual church-meeting in February 1847 the number of members was 116, after deducting all the deaths, dismissions, withdrawments, [96] exclusions, etc. This was I think the highest number it attained. Our Sunday school ran throughout very nearly parallel with the church: the number of children being at first fewer than twenty, latterly more than a hundred.

During the first six years of my pastorate the leading deacon and treasurer of the church was Mr. Philip Curtis, a lace dealer, who went to London regularly every month on business. This led him to believe that if I were to spend a week or ten days in the metropolis I should be able to collect something considerable towards the diminution of our chapel debt, and as the Rev. T. Allen usually spent his vacation month

---

20 The Rev. James Mursell became minister at Little Meeting, by then known as Fuller, in 1853, in succession to the Rev. William Robinson (J. K. Hall's successor).

in town, and was doing so in May 1825, and as Mr. Curtis felt sure that Mr. Allen would furnish me with the names and addresses of many persons likely to contribute, the church, without any wish on my part, voluntarily offered to defray [97] my expenses if I would consent to go. Accordingly on the 23rd of May, after a journey of nearly ten hours on the Kettering coach, I entered London for the first time. I well recollect that while on the coach in passing down one of the crowded streets we met a funeral procession. Ah! I thought Death takes off all the people here one by one as certainly as he does in the country! On Tuesday evening I heard the Rev. Edward Mannering preach, though I think not in his own chapel in Bishopsgate Street. Early on that day I purchased a four shilling map of London, and forthwith got the direction of the principal streets so clearly into my head that I have seldom been long at fault in finding my way from one part to another.

Being anxious to commence any work of collecting I called on Mr. Allen on Wednesday morning. On telling him my errand, the first question he asked was, "Is the trust deed of your Chapel enrolled in Chancery?" [98] I replied, "We have no trust deed, as the Church unanimously thought it neither needful nor desirable to incur the cost of one." "Then," said he, "you need not think of collecting money in London, for wherever you call, the first inquiry will be, 'Is your chapel enrolled?'" I confess I was glad to hear him express this belief. I did not like the thought of traversing London streets as a beggar, even in a good cause and had therefore reluctantly undertaken the mission and, moreover, had from the beginning entertained and expressed the opinion that if we thought proper to erect a chapel, we ought ourselves to pay for it; at any rate ought to do our utmost before asking aid from others.

Mr. Curtis had returned to Kettering, but previous to setting off had told me that if Mr. Allen did not give me sufficient assistance, it would be well to call on the Rev. Joseph Hinds, pastor of the Baptist Church at Sharnbrook, Bedfordshire, who would be in London on the following Monday. I did so, and found his belief [99] fully accorded with that of Mr. Allen. I therefore returned to Kettering on Tuesday the 31st, of course without having collected a shilling.

To myself, however, the time spent in London was far from being wasted. I rambled in the Parks, heard the barristers plead on behalf of certain Bills in the Committee Rooms of the House of Commons, visited Westminster Hall and Westminster Abbey; also the British Museum, Saint Paul's, the Tower of London, etc., etc., etc., ascended the Monument, went to Billingsgate Fish Market before six o'clock in the morning, and of course heard enough of the *patois* or slang of that notorious locality; walked to nearly the end of the Dog Row beyond Mile End Tollgate, and there called on a friend. Indeed, I spent the week so industriously that some of my friends said I had seen more of London in that week than they had in the twenty years they had resided there.

I had often wondered how masons laid the foundation of bridges beneath the [100] water and built the sterlings or piers before reaching the surface. I imagined they worked in diving bells, but on the Friday when crossing old London Bridge I saw a number of men preparing for the laying the foundation of the London Bridge now existing. I noticed that they worked in what is called a "Coffer Dam"; the said Coffer Dam consisting of a double ring of long and thick logs of deal, the logs in each ring or circle being placed side by side close to each other, each log being pointed at its low end and driven down into the clay by a steam hammer. The two circles being perhaps ten feet apart the intervening space was filled up with clay well rammed down, and when this clay wall was completed so as to be well nigh waterproof, the water in the centre was pumped out by a steam engine, and when all was pumped out of course the labourers had an opportunity of digging out the clay until they reached a basis sufficiently sound to sustain the weight of the bridge. I should not have learnt [101] all this had not a steam engine been there at work in driving down the piles of a Coffer Dam for a second pier. But looking attentively with both eyes I learnt enough in the few minutes I stood there to be able to give such a description of the process as has enabled my friends to understand it.

At seven o'clock one morning I heard a sermon preached in a chapel in the neighbourhood of Aldgate. On the morning of Sunday the 29th I heard the Rev. T. Price LL.D. preach in Devonshire Square chapel, where he was then pastor (he not having then lost his voice). In the afternoon I attended Dr. Rippon's chapel in Carter Lane, Tooley Street (on the completion of the new London Bridge that chapel was purchased and taken down for widening the approaches to the Bridge). I fully intended to hear the Rev. Edward Irving in the evening (who was then in the zenith of his popularity, or perhaps a little beyond the zenith), but after tea a person from Northamptonshire [102] having called to see the friend at whose house I was sojourning, persuaded me to go with him to hear his minister, Mr. Bailey, pastor of the Baptist Church in Great Alie Street, a step which I have always since regretted inasmuch as the sermon I heard was a very poor one, and I thus for ever lost the opportunity of hearing the celebrated though eccentric Irving.

When returning per the Kettering coach on Tuesday the 31st, a rather short, thin, wiry looking Quaker, apparently about seventy years old, got on the coach at Hitchin, and sat near to me until we reached

Higham Ferrers, the coach stopping to leave him at the house of Mr. Samuel Cook, a Quaker farmer, who afterwards married Mrs. Warner of Kettering and lived in our town for several years. I was deeply interested in the conversation of my fellow passenger. He told us he had been to Russia, and was in Saint Petersburg during the destructive floods which occurred there in [103] 1824, and that though the inhabitants were greatly alarmed during the danger, yet that the theatres were presently re-opened, and played as much as heretofore. I parted from him without learning his name, nor did I ascertain it until more than fifteen years afterwards, when I found he was none other than Thomas Shillitoe, the almost world-wide renowned Quaker missionary, of whom more hereafter.

I have omitted to say that in the beginning of March 1825 I, for the first time, attended the assizes at Northampton. Nearly the whole of the first day was occupied by an action at law respecting the ownership of a tree of the value of twelve shillings, the action, however, also involving the question of right to the ownership of the piece of land beneath and near to the said tree: the defendant satisfactorily showing that he and his ancestors had always claimed and lopped the tree in question, the plaintiff [104] contending and showing that from time immemorial the defendant's land had been bounded by the brook, which as the witness have proved flows at some distance from the tree. Both statements were correct. The fact being that during a somewhat recent flood the brook had excavated for itself a new permanent channel across the land of the defendant, thus leaving the tree some distance from the *present* stream. The verdict given was in accordance with this view. Plaintiff, the rector of Old; defendant, Mr. Knight, of either Hannington or Walgrave. The logical sparring and ready wit of the contending counsel, amused me not a little.

The trial of prisoners commenced on the following morning: and I thought the jury not sufficiently attentive to the evidence which was being laid before them, the proceedings, as a whole produced a solemn and not unprofitable effect on my mind. This led me to preach on the following Sunday [105] from Isaiah 53.8: in the afternoon from I Peter 4.12,13; in the evening II Corinthians 5.10.

In the end of July I had occasion to go into Bedfordshire on business. I rode to Higham Ferrers by coach, and, being always fond of walking, travelled on foot to Bedford, Shefford and Biggleswade: in the whole about thirty miles. On enquiring at an Inn whether I could sleep there the landlady said "If you would not object to a two bedded room we can accommodate you." I replied I had no objection thereto, little thinking that the Lord was about to teach me a lesson in that room which I should practically remember all my days. From the time of my beginning to seek salvation I had regularly knelt down to pray every night and morning: and therefore with that purpose retired somewhat early to my bedroom: but to my disappointment found that the other bed therein was already occupied by two men who were [106] evidently not asleep. I hesitated whether to kneel down or not, but the temptation to pray in bed instead of by its side assailed me and prevailed. I prayed before closing my eyes in slumber, but soon after five o'clock the next morning was made completely ashamed of my cowardice, for no sooner had I opened my eyes than I saw both the men who had occupied the other bed kneeling down by its side in prayer. I subsequently discovered that they were hawkers of Irish linen. I think they were Roman Catholics, but of that I am not certain.

I forthwith resolved in the Lord's strength that from that moment I would never anywhere, or under any circumstances again get into bed without first kneeling down to pray: a pledge which by His grace I have been enabled to redeem: for though I have occasionally had room mates and bedfellows, some of them members of Christian churches, and even ministers of Christ who [107] have omitted to kneel, I have never done so since that memorable night. And the advantage has not been restricted to myself alone. More than ten years afterwards a person of Warkton who had begun to seek the salvation of his soul, said to me, "Sir, I wish to ask you a question." "Very good," I replied, "What is it?" "Well, Sir," said he, "I have engaged myself to a farmer for the month of harvest. I know I shall have to sleep in a room with other men, some of them very reprobate characters. I am now in the habit of kneeling to pray before getting into bed. Will it be best to do so in the presence of those men who will very likely mock and ridicule me, or to pray after I lie down in bed?" In reply, I gave him a recital of my experience at Biggleswade, and of the resolution I then found. I believe he formed a similar resolve and carried it out practically.

Towards the close of that year, (1825), about sixteen young men of Kettering, most of them [108] members of Christian churches, formed themselves into what was called a "Debating Society", of which I was appointed secretary. It held its monthly meetings regularly for three years or upwards, in Ebenezer Chapel vestry (*viz.* the one in which I preached) and the Independent vestry being alternately our places of meeting. The following are some of the subjects discussed by us, "Is the existence of *different* denominations of Christians more or less conducive to the spread of true religion than *one* would be?" ... "Weight of character" ... "Was the death of Christ the death of his divinity or the death of merely his human nature? How is it possible for Deity to die? If only his human life expired how could his atonement have infinite merit?" "Have brutes souls?" … "Admitting the existence of a plurality of worlds, what reason have we to believe that any besides the earth are inhabited?" … "What reasons can be assigned for believing that Christians will [109] be able to recognize each other in a future state?" "What physical changes may be supposed to have occurred at the fall?" … "Does the phrase 'Son of God' as applied by inspired persons to Christ refer to his divine nature or his human nature?" … "Is the soul of a human being derived directly from God, or by traduction from the parents?" … "Wherein consists the true honour of man?" … "Is matter eternal? Was it created? Will it ever be annihilated?" … "Are those heathens lost who live and die without any knowledge of the Saviour?" "Will all the inhabitants of our world, at any time prior to the general judgement be true believers?" … "What are the best means we can adopt to obtain right ideas of God?" … "If the soul of Lazarus (or any other) during its absence from the body was in the world of unmingled holiness and joy, was not his resurrection an interruption of his blessedness?" In discussing questions like these [110] we, of course, presently found ourselves at the limits of our knowledge, nevertheless as exercises to our own mental powers the discussions were highly useful to us.

I believe it was in 1825 that a letter of mine pointing out the folly as well as the injustice of the course adopted by our West Indian slaveholders appeared in the *Northampton Mercury*, on which my relative referred to above [Robert Smith] complimented me by the remark that I had "hit the nail plump on the head." A response appearing in the next week's *Mercury*, I wrote a second letter in vindication and support of the first: and thus that matter ended.

The late John Cooper Gotch, Esq. shoe manufacturer and banker was one of the earliest and most cordial and steadfast friends of the Rev. J. K. Hall, and consequently strongly (perhaps not inexcusably) opposed to us [111] on account of our secession from the church. In consequence of the fearful commercial panic in December 1825, Mr. Gotch was compelled to suspend payment and to have his name enrolled in the *Gazette* list of bankrupts. This was an overwhelming trial to him, but the docket having been struck by one of his friends, payment of the dividends was wisely spread over about two years: which enabled the estate to pay twenty shillings in the pound to every creditor, and also interest on the amount owing to each. The Bank was therefore re-opened with re-established credit.

My acre of garden ground referred to above, was on its north side bounded by more than another acre of garden ground, no fence having been betwixt the two since the year 1784, though I have digged up some of the foundation of the wall which separated them previous

Figure 2. John Cooper Gotch (1772-1852), banker, wholesale footwear manufacturer, Kettering's leading figure in the first half of the nineteenth century, He was a deacon at Little Meeting and no friend of John Jenkinson. (*Author's collection*)

to that time. This northernmost part of the garden has been occupied by our family every since 1763: the owners being first [112] Thompson, (or, as that family spelt their surname, Tomson[21]) then Judkin, then Gotch. In consequence of Mr. Gotch's bankruptcy his estates were, of course, offered for sale. Within less than two hours of the advertisement in the *Northampton Mercury* having reached Kettering the late Mr. Thomas Dash, bookseller and printer, a very eccentric but a truly considerate and kind-hearted man, called on me, and said, "I have just seen an advertisement of a garden to be sold. I believe that garden is in your occupation." "Yes, sir," I replied, "it has been occupied by our family more than sixty two years." "I thought so," he rejoined. "Have you any thought of purchasing it?" "Yes Sir," I said. "O then my work is half done. On reading the advertisement at our breakfast table this morning, I said, it will be a hard case William, if a stranger should buy that garden, [113] and turn those people out of their business. I will go

21 [*A note by J.J.*] See the gravestones of Christopher Tomson, and of his son Kitt Tomson in Kettering churchyard, very near Woods Walk. They were relations of Adam Tomson of Oakham.

and ask Mr. Jenkinson if he thinks of buying it. If he does not, or cannot, I will buy it, and he shall be my tenant on the same terms as he has rented it of Mr. Gotch. If he thinks of purchasing it, and wants a friend to lend him the money, *I* will be that friend." "Thank you, Sir," I said "your offer is indeed a specially kind one, but another friend has offered to lend us whatever money we need to complete the purchase." Was not Mr. Dash's conduct on that occasion such as deservedly to embalm his name in my remembrance to the present hour? And although I did not *then* need to avail myself of his generous offer, yet when on the death of the friend who lent me £140 towards the purchase of the garden, I applied to Mr. Dash for the loan of £40, he forthwith complied with my request.

The failure of Kettering Bank in 1825 was therefore a means of pecuniary advantage [114] to me, for though I purchased the garden at a higher figure per acre than I believe had ever previously been asked for land in Kettering (except for building purposes) it has long since become worth more than twice as much as it cost me, and is every year increasing in value in consequence of the increase of the population of the town. The purchase was, moreover, favourable to my independency of action, inasmuch as it invested me with greater freedom of personal action both in religion and politics than I should like to have taken while tenant under Mr. Gotch.

In the month of February 1826 my beloved brother Edward was suddenly taken ill with Inflammation on the brain, commonly called "Brain Fever". Two tradesmen in the town who had the same disease in the course of that year, both died after a few days illness: and the medical attendant deemed my brother's case a very dangerous [115] one. I shall never forget my agony of mind during the continuance of his danger. On Sunday morning, February 19th, I preached from II Corinthians 4.17, in the afternoon from Matthew 26.39: in the evening from Job 4.3,4,5 "Behold, thou hast instructed many, and thou hast strengthened the weak hands. Thy words have upholden him that was falling, and thou has strengthened the feeble knees. But now it is come upon *thee*, and *thou* faintest; it toucheth thee, and thou art troubled." But an ever-gracious God was better to me than my fears. By shaving the head of the dear sufferer, applying a blister thereto, assiduous nursing, the skill of the medical adviser, and above all by the Lord's blessing on the use of these means, my dear brother was enabled to weather the storm. The doctor calling to see whilst I was preaching on Sunday evening, the nurse met him on the stairs, and whispered, "he is fast asleep, Sir." On hearing which he instantly turned, and, descending the stairs said, "O, I am so glad he is sleeping: that will do him more good than all my medicine." The crisis being thus passed, he presently began to recover, though, of course, he continued very weak for some time. On Sunday the 26th my glad and grateful heart prompted me to preach from Psalms 116.1,2, which I did with happier feelings than those of the preceding Sabbath.

On the 24th of January 1826 I for the first time preached in my native village, [Hallaton], and did so again on October 17th: on both which occasions my schoolmaster, Mr. Buzzard (see page 9), who, I was told, had never previously entered a Dissenting Chapel, was present to hear me, as he also was on the one or two subsequent times I preached at Hallaton prior to his death. On leaving the chapel after hearing the first time he said to one of my friends, "Mr. Jenkinson would not have preached so well if he had not come to [117] my school!"

On the 23rd of March 1826, the universal waster, Death, for the first time invaded our church: taking from us a poor but pious person named Hannah Roughton. Her remains were brought into our chapel previous to interment, and on Sunday afternoon April 2nd, I preached a funeral sermon for her from Isaiah 60.20: "The days of thy mourning shall be ended."

The summer of 1826 was the hottest and driest in my remembrance. The crop of hay was consequently very, *very* scanty. The price of hay presently became ruinously high to its purchasers: and the unusual backwardness of the ensuing Spring, rendered it a very trying time to many. A friend of mine (the late Mr. James Longland, of Grendon) who sent butter to the London market, and for that purpose kept twenty-eight cows, told me that [118] if he had given them all away at Michaelmas 1826, he should have saved money by doing so: for though they did not all actually die, they, notwithstanding his purchasing hay for them at an unprecedented price, many of them became so emaciated in constitution as to be worth very little afterwards.

I frequently preached at Broughton and Cransley. Having done so on Lord's day September 17th, 1826, a person of Kettering a few days afterwards asked me what I preached from at Broughton on Sabbath evening. "From I John 5.10," I replied, "Why," said he, "I have been told that you said you had no doubt there are children in hell not a span long!" "Well," I said, "I have heard that falsehood two or three times in months gone by, though all who have heard me regularly know that I have never uttered anything approaching thereto, and I am conscious that I never had even a thought in that direction [119] but I will hear the slander no more." I therefore on the next Lord's day gave public notice in my chapel that by the Lord's will I should on the following Sunday evening October 1st, preach a sermon, "On the certain salvation of all who die in infancy," which I accordingly did. Our chapel was crowded on the occasion, and on the Monday several of my friends expressed their wish that the sermon should be printed, and one of Mr. Hall's regular hearers said he was so pleased with it that he would give a sovereign towards the cost. All that I had written of it previous to preaching it is now lying before me, and is scarcely larger than the palm of my hand. But I set to work to write it out in full, and ere long sent it to the press. Of the five hundred copies printed I have for nearly thirty-five years past had only a solitary copy left, and could have repeatedly sold *that* at a greatly enhanced price. The failure of my London publisher deprived me of nearly [120] all pecuniary profit from the venture, my receipts for copies sold in other quarters being very little more than sufficient to defray the cost of printing, which was somewhat large.[22]

In his *Life of Kirke White*, Dr. Southey says of that excellent poet, "He would not have vexed himself to death over a review if he had been reviewed sixty nine times as I have." Being, like Kirke White, inexperienced in such matters, I greatly dreaded the scalping knife of the reviewers, and therefore sent copies of my sermon, if I rightly recollect, only to the *Baptist* and *New Baptist Magazine*. Amongst other commendatory remarks the first named says:

> "Had we not known that the author of this sermon was young in the ministry and self-educated, we should not have conjectured either from this (we believe) his first publication … Had our limits permitted we should have gladly given a specimen of the author's perspicuous style, and nervous reasoning. [121] We most heartily recommend it as one of the most useful sermons that have lately been published."
> (*Baptist Magazine* June 1827)

The Rev. William Jones, editor of the *New Baptist Miscellany*, was well-known to be a severe and merciless critic. My friends were therefore scarcely more pleased than surprized to read the favourable critique from which the following is an extract:

> "With the author of this sermon we are wholly unacquainted, indeed his name had scarcely reached us, when it was placed in our hands. Our surprize and pleasure have therefore been considerable, in discovering in it much acuteness of thought, clothed in an easy and flowing style … We can most cordially

---

22 *On the Certain Salvation of all who die in Infancy. Sermon preached at the New Baptist Meeting in Kettering. By John Jenkinson, 1826.*

recommend it to our readers, as calculated to rejoice their hearts when suffering under the bereaving dispensations of providence." (*New Baptist Miscellany*, October 1827)

[122]   These reviews, and especially the sermon itself, gained me friends in various parts of the country: the slander specified on page 118 was thus amongst all the things which worked together for my good.

[*A temporary crisis of faith*]

The week commencing April the 8th, 1827, was a memorable one in my experience. Nearly the whole of that Sabbath was a happy one to me. A young friend from Nottingham, whom I did not previously know to be piously inclined, prayed with us at our morning prayer meeting at seven o'clock. This gave me great pleasure. At half past ten I preached from I Samuel 22.2; in the afternoon from Joshua 5.14. Went to Isham to preach in the evening. Enjoyed all the services very much. The pious friend referred to above on page 93 accompanied me more than a mile on my return. When parting with him I said, "Well, we must part again, and we shall one day have to part for the last time. Shall we meet in [123] heaven?" His reply was in accordance with this remark. On leaving him, and pursuing my way homeward alone, my thoughts immediately and vividly dwelt on the moment after death and the solemn realities connected therewith. In an agony of soul I cried out "O God, O God, shall I then find myself saved or lost?" The more I pondered this momentous question, the more was my hope eclipsed by fear. Before reaching home my agony was so great that I could think of no words adapted to my case except "groanings which cannot be uttered." My distress of soul continued throughout the week. On the Monday a young friend said to me, "You seem to be in trouble." I replied, "I *am* in trouble." I then told him how the train of my thoughts had led me to the borders of despair. He said, "You forget what you told me in your sermon yesterday morning that the believer in all his discontent with himself and distress about sin or anything else has an almighty, an ever wise [124] and ever-gracious Friend to whom he can repair, and that he goes to him and follows and obeys him as his Captain." "Ah!" I said. "But I fear I am *not* a believer."

I had on Saturday chosen Hebrews 2.10. as my text for the next Wednesday evening: but instead of discoursing from it in the way I first intended, I dwelt on it chiefly in reference to Christ as the Captain of salvation being "made perfect through suffering" a view which of course most harmonized with the then state of my own mind. This sermon somewhat relieved my agony, though it still continued.

As Easter Day was on the following Sunday I had some difficulty in fixing on a text of a sermon which should combine the gladness appropriate to the Redeemer's resurrection with the gloom in which my own mind was enveloped. At length, Luke 24.17 occurred to me as presenting matter suitable to both. I therefore preached therefrom [125] on Sunday morning, and from the 30th and 31st verses of the same chapter in the afternoon, the Lord's supper being regularly administered at our chapel on the third Sabbath in the month. While I preached these two sermons my cries for deliverance from my grief and fear were answered, the storm ceased, the clouds were dispersed, and I again began to go on my way rejoicing.

Awfully painful as that week was, it was nevertheless one of the most profitable in my life. I had previously been often strongly tempted to infidelity, but have never been thus tempted since. In that week I *felt* the Bible to be true, for its teachings and its threatenings were like a sharp two-edged sword in my soul. I felt there was a heaven, and feared I had lost it, I felt there was a hell, and was well-nigh certain I was doomed to it. In that week I bitterly learnt the truth of Newton's exquisite hymn:

[126]

"I asked the lord that I might grow
"In faith, and love, and every grace,
"Might more of his salvation know,
"And seek more earnestly his face.

"'Twas he who taught me thus to pray
"And he, I trust, has answered prayer,
"But it has been in such a way
"As almost drove me to despair.

"I hop'd that in some favoured hour
"At once he'd answer my request,
"And by his love's constraining power
"Subdue my sins, and give me rest

"Instead of this, he made me feel
"The hidden evils of my heart
"And let the angry powers of hell
"Assault my soul in every part.

"Lord! why is this? I trembling cried,
"Will thou pursue thy worm to death?
[127]
"'Tis in this way, the Lord replied
"I answer prayer for grace and faith."

On June the 8th I again preached at Hallaton, my native village. The next morning I called on an old neighbour, who with his wife were avowed Antinomians,[23] a church of that denomination having long existed in the village. In the course of our conversation he said, "Were you not wrong in your sermon last night?" "In what respect?" I asked "Why," he replied, "you spoke about David's praying. David never prayed. The Lord's people never pray. Christ prays *for* them, and, as he is infinitely wiser than they, there is no need for them to pray. The psalms do not contain any prayers of David, but Christ's prayers for himself and for his people." To which his wife added, "And folks talk about holiness too. We want no personal holiness. Christ is all the holiness [128] we need!" I have since acquired reason to believe that for a long time previous to their marriage they had practically lived in accordance with this creed. After pointing out what I deemed their dangerous error I parted with them, and saw them no more. I was pleased to learn from the leading member of the Baptist Church in Hallaton, that the man gave satisfactory evidence of genuine repentance before his death: but, alas! this cheering information was chequered by the further statement that the woman died as she had lived.

The above recorded visit to Hallaton was on a weekday, but in the following month (July 29th, 1827) I preached there on a Sabbath, and stayed until Tuesday. On awaking betwixt four and five o'clock on Monday morning I heard the sound of distant thunder, but did not imagine the mischief the storm was doing. As it did not come near to Hallaton I thought very little of it until [129] the afternoon, when a report spread through the village that some houses at *Ketton* had been set on fire by the lightning and burnt down. In less than an hour afterwards the report was corrected from "Ketton" to "Kettering". This, of course, occasioned me some concern, as I thought the houses which were burnt might be my own. However, I consoled myself with the thought that as my houses were not in the highest part of Kettering they most likely had escaped. Under the influence of that thought, and trusting myself and all my affairs in the Lord's hands, I enjoyed a good night's rest, and, leaving Hallaton immediately after breakfast on Tuesday, I walked to Kettering and reached it about one o'clock. There my brother Edward told me that he was gathering fruit in his garden a little after four o'clock on Monday morning when a thunder storm suddenly came on, and three of the most terrific thunder-crashes he ever heard or [130] imagined occurred at intervals of two or three minutes, each crash being instantly accompanied by a fearful flash of lightning: the first of which struck a tree in Chater's Park, about 250 yards west of

23 Calvinists who maintained that the moral law was not binding upon the Elect under the law of grace.

him, and split a tree from the collar to the ground, the second flash killed a child in a house near the top of Goosepasture Lane (now Gas Street) about the same distance south of him, set the house on fire, the whole range of four houses being thereby burnt down, the third flash struck the toll-gate house on the road to Barton-Seagrave, rent the wall from the top to the bottom, ran round the curtain rods of the bed on which part of the family were sleeping, shivered one of the bedposts (a splinter of which is now lying before me) but providentially, though eight persons were in bed in the house, no one of them was hurt.

On descending Warren Hill at dinner time on Tuesday I wondered why so many persons were going into Chater's Park, but [131] presently learnt that they were going to look at the stricken tree. Since that time I have often thought what an almost miracle of mercy it was that my dear brother was not killed by the electric fluid which in its destructive course passed so near to him, and to which the very lofty pear tree beneath which he was gathering gooseberries might have been a likely conductor.

My friend, the Rev. T. Allen had preached for me on the Sunday, and announced his willingness to comply with the request made to him that he would preach on Monday evening. Some of my people told me that a large congregation assembled on that evening in the full expectation of hearing some reference to the thunderstorm and the fire, but to their great disappointment not a word was said about either.

[*Giving up market gardening for the full-time ministry*]
For nearly four years after [132] the commencement of my pastorate I continued in business, the said business (that of market gardening) being one, which beyond most others, required ceaseless care and management, and assiduous personal manual toil of a very laborious kind. My difficulty, however, arose neither from the mental labour of preparing for the pulpit, nor from the toilsome physical labour of cultivating the heavy soil of which the garden largely consisted, but from the intensity of my love to both: their claims on me being often incompatible with each other. My ardent love of my business led me never to wish to spend an hour of a weekday out of the garden, and my ardent love to my ministerial work leading me to neglect no opportunity of preaching either at home or elsewhere. The first sometimes when working led me to regret I had made preaching engagements which would take me from my business for one or more days: and when from home [133] the second led me to regret that I had not more time to devote to my preaching, and preparation for it. But the feeling grew upon me that the world must yield to Christ, things earthly to things heavenly. Consequently, on the approach of my brother

Edward's marriage, I proposed to him that he should become my tenant and my successor in the business. We had no trouble in agreeing as to the terms, and though more than forty years have passed since that agreement was made it has never been altered, nor even excited a wish for an alteration in either of our minds. During my wedded life my other half sometimes spoke as if she thought the rent too small (which perhaps it is) but assuredly I never thought of increasing it.

On December 26th, 1827, my brother was married [to Avis Fairey] in Ringstead parish church (Dissenters being at that time precluded from having the marriage services performed in their churches). [134] I accompanied him for the purpose of giving away the bride. Our journey from Kettering was literally through the darkness and the deeps. We started from home before daylight, and after travelling nearly six miles, we met a person who told us the flood was so great he did not think we should be able to get across Ringstead meadows, but as we had not time to go round by Thrapston we kept on our way, and as a consequence got nearly up to our waists in water. However, on reaching Ringstead we presently dried our clothes, and were at church quite in time to have the marriage celebrated within the canonical hours. I preached in Ringstead Baptist Chapel in the evening, and returned home on the following day.

I have omitted to state that at the ordination of Mr. Tanday as pastor of the Baptist Church at Great Gidding [Cambridgeshire] on the [135] last day of May 1826 and at the ordination of Mr. Manton as pastor of the Baptist Church at Oundle on August 7th, 1827, I preached in the evening. Of course, on each occasion, several ministers were present. On the first Sunday in 1828 I preached at Little Staughton, Beds, and made my home at the house of a gentleman named Goodliffe, who was not a decided Christian: of whom more hereafter.

On the second Sunday in May I preached the annual sermons on behalf of the Baptist Sunday School at Ringstead. On the 29th of July I preached in the General Baptist Chapel, Loughborough [Leicestershire], in which town three dissenting chapels were then being built. The old Wesleyan Chapel being not capable of seating more than 700 persons, the people who worshipped therein had resolved to erect one capable of seating 1,000. The General Baptist Chapel in which I preached would seat 900, and it having for many years [136] been the largest in the town, its attendants did not relish being put second, they therefore resolved to erect one capable of holding 1,200. The Independents having theretofore had no place of worship in the town, resolved to build one. Thus it occurred that the three chapels were built simultaneously. I was subsequently told, I know not how truly, that the

Wesleyans being anxious to secure the first gleaning of the field, vigorously pushed on the completion of *their* chapel, so as to have it opened in November, which was done, the total collections at the services being £160. The General Baptists had *theirs* opened on Christmas Day and the Sunday following, the total of *their* collections being about £500.

The Baptist Chapel at Oundle having been extensively repaired, I was requested to preach at its re-opening, which I did on Sunday August 24th. On returning home on the following day, I and a young friend who accompanied me called on the Rev. D. Parkins, Baptist Minister, who frequently [137] preached at Kettering when Mr. Hall was from home. In the course of our conversation Mr. Parkins expressed his regret at the continuance of the hostility betwixt myself and Mr. Hall. I assured him that there was no hostility on my part. To which he replied, "I believe I may confidently say there is none on the part of Mr. Hall." I therefore in the course of that week wrote a very respectful letter to Mr. Hall, in which I expressed my sincere regret for everything which had offended him: the whole letter being one which I think no one could justly condemn, except perhaps for its extreme humility and penitence. Instead, however, of eliciting a kind rejoinder from Mr. Hall he reiterated all the old charges against me, most of them being utterly unfounded [see Appendix 1]. I did not demean myself to return a reply but on October 22nd circumstances occurred, which are sufficiently narrated in my pamphlet entitled *Kettering*[24] (in which every charge in the above named letter is answered) to which the reader who desires further information may have recourse. [138] On the very next morning I and several friends went to the ordination of Mr. Liddell as pastor of the Baptist Church at Hallaton (my native village). Leaving our conveyance at Medbourne until the evening, we walked the two miles to Hallaton. My mind being somewhat agitated by the occurrences of the previous day. I loitered behind my companions, and while doing so, a member, I believe a deacon of the Independent church at Wilbarston, having walked from thence joined me at the junction of the two roads. On conversing with him he said, "You are a stranger to me. May I ask your name?" On my informing him he replied, "O I heard of you in Bedfordshire: to which county I sometimes go to buy timber, and was there in February last." I said, "I preached at Staughton on the first Sunday in this year, and made my home with a gentleman named Goodliffe, who on Monday morning walked with me nearly to Kimbolton. Though then in perfect health he died about a month

---

24 This was *A Letter to John Cooper Gotch, Esquire, Containing a Reply to every Allegation Advanced by the Revd. J. K. Hall A.M. against the Author*. This, in turn, was replied to in a pamphlet by George Wallis, *A Letter to J. C. Gotch, Esquire, of Kettering, Occasioned by Mr. Jenkinson's Letter*, 1829, reiterating the case against Jenkinson in the secession.

afterwards." [139] "Yes," he replied, "I was there at the time of his death, and went to hear the sermon which was preached in reference to it. I was told that your sermons on the Sunday, and your conversation with him when walking on the Monday, evidently produced a deep and favourable impression on his mind." Having by this time overtaken my companions my conversation with the stranger terminated, but I throughout the day admired the kindness and wisdom of God in thus unexpectedly sending me so sweet an antidote to my trouble.

At the ordination, the Rev. J. K. Hall, of Kettering, asked the usual questions and received Mr. Liddell's confession of faith. The charge was given by Mr. Liddell's pastor, the Rev. T. Morgan of Birmingham, whom I then met for the first time. After the service, the ministers, deacons, etc. dined together at the *Bewicke Arms*. Amongst those present were the Revs. W. Liddell, T. Morgan, J. Mack, J. K. Hall and myself; no one in [140] the company imagining that Mr. Hall and myself had had a public fracas not eighteen hours before.

A vexing circumstance occurred on our return. My father-in-law [*i.e.* step-father] (who was of a somewhat unlovely temper) being, I suppose, displeased that so many of us had gone in the conveyance gratuitously lent him, set off and walked to Medbourne (taking my mother with him) an hour earlier than the time fixed in the morning. We thought surely he would wait for us at Medbourne, but when we reached that village he and my mother and the conveyance were gone. We could hear the sound of the wheels about a mile distant, and therefore hurried across the meadows by a footpath to Cottingham (nearly five miles from Medbourne). We felt certain that the fleetest of us would reach Cottingham before the arrival of the conveyance, and thus be able to stop it until our companions had overtaken us. And we should have done, had not the artful man for the purpose of avoiding us returned to Kettering by another way than the one we had gone in the morning. Both male and female had consequently to walk the whole of the sixteen miles to Kettering, which we did not reach until after midnight. We intended to give our charioteer a handsome donation: but he so grievously disappointed us, that he did not receive even our thanks.

The writing of my pamphlet, and waiting at Northampton while it was printed employed all my time during the next fortnight.

Early in 1829, one of Mr. Hall's deacons (Mr. George Wallis, a truly excellent man) published a reply to my pamphlet, evidently not wholly his own production. My first edition being presently exhausted, and a second one demanded I inserted a brief appendix in answer to

Mr. Wallis [Appendix 1]. Meanwhile, the health of Mr. Hall had gradually declined, [142] until on April 18th, he exchanged earth for heaven, to which within a few weeks he was followed by his warm partisan, Mrs. Waters, my mother's sister, one of my most inveterate opponents, but who, previous to her death, sent for me, not to reprove or blame me, but with whom I had some very pleasant and profitable conversation.

In consequence of my pamphlet, a kind old lady at Broughton in whose barn I had frequently preached on Lord's day evenings, for four years past, except in the depth of winter, refused to allow me to come to it any more. But one of my members having thereupon licensed his house for preaching, the exclusion did me small injury, and having some Sabbath evenings unengaged which otherwise I should not have had, I preached in the open air at Warkton, Weekley, Grafton and other villages in which the gospel had not for many many years been heard, and in all of which my labours were blessed, sinners converted, prayer meetings established, [143] and houses presently licensed for preaching. Thus, good resulted from evil, and lo! the very next spring the old lady above referred to sent me word that I should be welcome to re-occupy her barn whenever I pleased. The fact was, many members of my church resided at Broughton and Cransley, and a considerable number of the inhabitants of each village were always glad to hear me, so that our congregations there were never small.

In May 1829, my friend Mr. J. Ashby (one of the young men referred to on page 107) in the course of conversation said, "When at Bedford last week I learnt that they have a manuscript magazine there. Could we not have one at Kettering?" I replied, "I think we could." I strongly pressed him to become its Editor, but this he positively declined, and urged me to undertake the office. To this I reluctantly consented, and issued the first number on July 1st, 1829, and without intermission continued the work for exactly twenty years: [144] and even at the expiration of that time it ceased only in consequence of my removal from Kettering to Oakham [see Appendix 2]. Mr. Ashby furnished several excellent articles: and having in 1830 become a student in Newport Pagnell College,* he procured me contributions from the Rev. S. Hillyard, Jun., now and for more than thirty years past pastor of the Congregational church at Bedworth, the Rev. J. Willis, long pastor at Lavenham [Suffolk], the Rev. T. Boaz, afterwards D.D. and long a missionary at Calcutta, etc. Some other friends also occasionally contributed, the most frequent being λαμβδα (*Lambda*, Mr. Leatherland),

---

* [*A note by J.J.*] The Rev. John Ashby himself was successively pastor at Brackley, Thetford and Stony Stratford.

but throughout the twenty years nearly all the magazine, and very often entirely all, had to be written by me. To this, however, I have always been grateful, inasmuch as it compelled me to think for myself on very many subjects to which my attention would probably not otherwise have been directed.

[145] In the last week of May 1829, the first Kettering Co-operative Society was established at a crowded meeting held in the Grammar School. I was utterly unexpectedly to myself appointed treasurer; I continued to hold that office until my removal to Oakham in June 1849. I regularly presented my financial report every three months, and repeatedly told the Auditors that for every penny of error they could discover, I would give them a sovereign. They looked keenly for mistakes, but I well knew they could not find any for I kept the accounts in such a way that if there was the smallest error in my book or the secretary's it could not fail to meet me when making out my Report. The secretary was James Toseland, an operative silkweaver: one of the most pious and intelligent working-men I ever knew. We often had a long conversation at the close of our monthly business meetings.

On Friday June 12th, I preached the annual sermon at the yearly meeting of a Friendly Society at Carlton, Beds, Text Eccles. 4.9-12. [146] In March 1830 I had a week of the severest illness I have ever known (a kind of sore throat fever). Mr. York, of Cransley, on of my deacons, called to see me on the Friday before leaving, he said, "What shall we do on Sunday?" I replied, "O I shall preach on Sunday." He thought me so ill that he was astonished to see me at chapel on the Lord's day. But though present I did not preach in the morning, as one of the deacons read a sermon. That being the only Lord's day service in my life in which sickness prevented me from preaching. In the afternoon I conducted the service, and preached as usual.

Having long had an ardent desire to see the sea, and to know more of a few of the eastern counties, I at the end of June 1830 took a pedestrian tour through some parts of Huntingdonshire, Cambridge, Norfolk and Lincoln. Walked to Peterborough on the Monday. Traversed that city, and went to the top of the Cathedral on Tuesday morning. Thence, by packet boat to [147] Wisbeach. Then walked to King's Lynn, and slept there. Fully intended to sail by packet to Boston, but learnt that there was no packet thither on Wednesdays. I therefore took a cruise in a ferry boat down the mouth of the river Ouse. Landed at some distance down the coast. Walked from thence by Sutton Wash, though Long Sutton, Fleet, Holbeach, Spalding to Deeping: being a walk on a hot summer's day of full forty miles. Next day, (Thursday) walked through Stamford, Collyweston, Duddington, Bulwick, Weldon, and

Geddington to Kettering, being about thirty four miles for the fourth day's journey; having by the good hand of God walked more than 120 miles since Monday morning without harm or great weariness.

Although I had preached three sermons on the previous Sunday in reference to the death of the King (George IV), the first announcement which I *saw* of his demise, was a placard on the wall of *Kate's Cabin* Inn where the road from Oundle to Peterborough crosses the Great [148] North Road. When conversing with a farmer on Wednesday morning near his lodge in the parish of, I believe, Tidd St Giles, he said, "Do you see that building in the distance yonder?" I replied "Yes." "Well," he replied, "that is Cromer Lighthouse: it is fifty miles from hence, yet several times when on a winter's night I have been coming home from our village I have thought that light was in my own house!"

Of course I was not then an abstainer from intoxicating drink. I left Lynn about six o'clock in the morning without staying for breakfast, fully believing that I should easily be able to obtain a glass of ale, or at least a draught of water, on my journey. The boatmen landed me about 400 yards from an embankment (or dike, as I believe it is called) raised for reclaiming the land from the sea, and truly told me that if I kept along that I should find [it] continued all the way to Sutton Washway. I therefore kept walking on mile after mile, and hour after [149] hour, being almost melted by the heat of the day and parched with an all but unendurable thirst. Many little pools of clean looking, sparkling water sometimes presented themselves near the foot of the embankment, but on descending for the purpose of allaying my thirst, I found the water as salty as brine. It was, in fact, seawater left by the receding tide in the hollows of the sand. Now and then I met a human being, and eagerly asked, "Can you tell me where I can get a drink of water?" "There is no fresh water near here," was the response. "Can I procure a glass of ale?" "Yes, at Sutton Washway Boathouse." "How far is that?" "About six miles further." I had therefore no alternative but to keep pushing forward: by which means I at last reached the said Boathouse, about three o'clock in the afternoon. The house was a wooden one, standing on four strong pillars. I believe at flood tide its floor was nearly level with the water, but at ebb several steps had to be ascended. Mounting these I found the house [150] nearly filled with customers. Finding a vacant seat, I called for a glass of ale. Almost fainting with thirst I thought every minute ten, but after waiting a considerable time no ale was brought to me. I said, "I asked for a glass of ale." "We don't sell ale," was the astounding reply. "Why," I rejoined, "I have been walking for more than eight hours without being able to procure a drop of anything to drink, and have repeatedly been told by persons whom I meet that I should be able to obtain some here." "We sell nuts", said the landlady, and if you buy three halfpennyworth of nuts we will give you a glass of ale" (I thence inferred that it was an *unlicensed* house). "Then bring three halfpenny worth of nuts aye bring me threepennyworth," I said. Accordingly about a dozen nuts and a pint jug of ale were speedily before me. Having drunk the ale, I had yet another glass, this being one of the only two occasions in which I had three glasses of ale at the same time.

Sutton Washway is at the mouth of the [151] river Nene, which is fordable there at low tide. I expected to reach it a low water, but when five or six miles off I both heard and saw the tide rolling in in the distance. As I was ascending the boathouse steps a man was attempting to ford the river, and had I think got half way across, but the water was nearly up to his breast, and the tide was rapidly rolling in: the boatman incessantly and loudly shouting, "Come back, Come back: you will be drowned." I believe this cry arose as much from regard to their interest as to the man's safety. However, the man deemed it prudent to return, and he and I went over together in the ferry boat, from which the Boathouse derives its name.

On March 14th, 1831, Death deprived me of the society and counsels of my highly valued friend, the Rev. T. Allen (see page 92). Though truly united in heart we never concealed from each other that our theological views were on some points dissimilar, he on the whole [152] agreeing with Dr. Gill, I with Mr. Fuller.[25] He was a man of considerable talent, and usually had a large congregation to hear him. During his pastorate his chapel was much enlarged, and also a good dwelling house for the pastor erected at no great distance therefrom. The last time I saw him was on Monday January 17th, on my return from Rushden, where I had supplied on the previous day. He had long suffered from gallstones, and was unwell when I called on him. His indisposition inducing a depression of spirits, he was a good deal cast down by some local circumstances which had occurred, and especially so by the fact that Earl Fitzwilliam had a few weeks previously presented the Rev. R. A. Hannaford (at that time a highly popular clergyman) to the living of Irthlingborough, which Mr. Allen foreboded would diminish *his* congregation, and thus prevent him from providing for his family. I said, "Leave all that in the Lord's [153] hands, and He will provide." On that day eight weeks, he had passed into eternity in the 49th year of his age. And the cloud he had dreaded proved in reality to be lined with mercy. The new vicar courteously called on Mr. Allen, and being somewhat skilled in medicine prescribed for his relief, which

---

25 Andrew Fuller, who, in his *Gospel of Christ Worthy of all Acceptation*, (1785), argued against the "Hyper- Calvinism" of Dr. John Gill (1697-1771), a London minister, and a native son of Kettering.

led to a repetition of his visit. When Death had left Mrs. Allen a widow and her children fatherless, the vicar kindly originated a subscription for their benefit, to which through his influence some other clergymen and Episcopalian laymen contributed, and Mr. Allen's dissenting friends in Irthlingborough, London, and elsewhere rendering their aid, the handsome sum of £200 was raised, which was invested for the use of the bereaved widow and family: an incident which tends to enforce upon us all the wise and needful counsel,

> "Judge not the Lord by feeble sense,
> "But trust Him for his grace
> "Behind a frowning providence
> "He hides a smiling face."

[154] On May 18th I attended the public meetings of the Newport Pagnell College Anniversary, on which occasion an admirable sermon was preached by the Rev. T. Raffles, D.D. of Liverpool. Text Luke 15.10.

My friend, the Rev. J. Whittemore, subsequently the projector, proprietor and editor of the *Christian World*, the *Sunday School Times*, the *Baptist Messenger*, etc. was ordained pastor of the first Baptist Chapel at Rushden, on June 14th, 1832, on the evening of which day I preached there to a very large congregation with great liberty and acceptance.

Of course, in common with the mass of my fellow citizens I felt a deep interest in the process of the Reform Bill, and attended several meetings in our town in reference thereto, especially when in the beginning of May 1832 the Tories attempted to regain the reins of power. This attempt having been happily frustrated I had the pleasure of taking part in the splendid public procession [155] and festivities by which the final passing of the Bill was celebrated in Kettering on June 19th, 1832. The motto on the Gardeners' banner, *Judicious Pruning Renovates the Tree*, was from my pen.

At the first election held at Kettering, December 15th, 1832, betwixt a thousand and twelve hundred Tory horsemen from all parts of North Northamptonshire entered the town in procession and took their standing mounted in front of the hustings.[26] As I stood at the door of one of my friends to see this cavalcade pass by, as they still kept coming and coming, apparently without end, my friend exclaimed "Oh,

---

26 This was the first election for which Kettering, under the recent Reform Act, was the polling place for a new constituency, Northamptonshire North. The first few general elections there were very heated.

what shall we do against all these?" This query suggested my sermon for the following morning from "Alas! My master, how shall we do?" II Kings 6.14-17. The sermon had, however, only a slight direct reference to the political excitement then pervading this division of the county.

Early in the year 1833 I was requested to supply the then destitute Baptist [156] Church in Little Wild Street, London, of which Drs. Samuel and Joseph Stennett, and the Rev. Joseph Hughes, one of the warm hearted Welshmen who originated the British and Foreign Bible Society, and of which he was one of the first Secretaries, had formerly been pastors. In compliance with this request I preached there on five successive Lord's days in April & May, also on three or four weekday evenings. At the close of my engagement, an unanimous and pressing invitation was given to me by the church to become its pastor: an invitation seconded by urgent letters from some leading members of other Baptist churches in London. This caused me much of anxious thought and led me to often and earnestly implore the guidance of the Infinitely Wise. The receipt of a whole packet of letters from Kettering entreating me not to leave, united with my sense of moral obligation in reference to our chapel debt, led me eventually to decline to accept the invitation, though I was then, and had all along been [157] preaching without any salary whatever.

That this decision did not fail to exert an influence favourable to Christianity is evident from what was said to one of my deacons by a leading infidel in the town. "I do think," said he, "that there must be something in religion, after all. I have always thought that Ministers preach only for what they get by it, but your minister has preferred to preach for nothing, rather than receive a good salary."

In addition to my services at Wild Street, I preached at Spencer Place, Eagle Street, (now King Street) Shoreditch, Devonshire Square, attended a Baptist Missionary meeting at Camberwell, etc., etc., etc. During my stay I, of course, came into occasional contact with several leading Baptist ministers and laymen, and repeatedly shared the hospitality of Messrs. Paxton, Millard, Haddon, Saunders, etc. My home was with Mr. Boulton, afterwards for several years a Baptist minister in South Africa.

[158] In the course of the many conversations I had with the leading deacon (Mr. Paxton, solicitor) respecting the future of the church, he said, "Mr. Wollacott, of Romney Street has had a division in his church, and has applied for the tenancy of our chapel. He will bring 58 of his members with him." "And why not let him have it?" I asked. "Because," said Mr. Paxton "he is somewhat higher in sentiment than

we are." "Perhaps so," I replied, "and yet probably he is not higher than those who built your chapel. My advice," I said, "is this: Let Mr. Wollacott and his friends rent the chapel off you for one year. If you and your friends do not like his preaching you can then terminate the tenancy. If you and your friends can hear him profitably you can at the end of the year invite him to become your pastor." This advice was happily adopted. Mr. Wollacott was heard and approved, received an invitation and accepted it, and continued to hold the pastorate for thirty years. Having [159] attained the age of seventy five he resigned his office at the end of 1863, "amidst the sincere regret of every member, and the sympathy and regard of a large circle of friends" (*Christian World* November 27th 1863).

In the year 1834 the British School-Rooms were built in Kettering. A musical festival took place therein on the first of August (the day when slavery was *nominally* abolished throughout the British Empire), and the schools were first opened for instruction of children on October 20th. Having in proportion to my means contributed towards their erection, I was appointed a member of the Managing Committee, an office to which I was re-appointed through several successive years.

Kettering Gasworks were erected in the same year. An unusually heavy pressure being placed on the gasworks, the town was splendidly lighted up on the evening of the opening, October 31st, 1834. On the following Sunday evening (November 2nd), I preached from Psalms CV, latter part 39: "Fire to give light in the night."

[160] On the last day in August 1834 four of my friends residing in Kettering and its vicinity went to Deenethorpe for the purpose of distributing religious tracts, conversing with the inhabitants of the village, and conducting public worship in the open air. Scarcely had they commenced the service ere Mr. Bingley, the constable of the parish, attended by several ungodly labouring men, pounced upon them, dragged them down the village street, and across one or two fields, until having reached a brook which probably bounds the lordship, they were let go. On the Monday morning they applied to a clerical magistrate of Kettering for redress, but instead of telling them, as he ought to have done, that they could summon the parties for assault, he asked whether the place where they were worshipping was licensed. "No sir," they replied, "it was in the open air." "Oh, then I can do nothing," he said, and so dismissed the case. They therefore forthwith came to me to ask what I thought would be the best course for them to pursue. I replied, "My advice is that you go again to Deenethorpe [161] next Sunday. Distribute tracts at every house, and tell all the people that by the Lord's

will I shall preach there at six o'clock on the Sunday following, on the very spot from which the constable dragged you." They did so. But it seemed an adverse occurrence that on Wednesday, September 10th, Adam Corrie, Esq. of Wellingborough wrote to request me to supply at Salem chapel in that town on the 14th. I answered that I should have been happy to comply with his request, but that I was under an engagement to preach at Deenethorpe in the evening (narrating the circumstances already stated). In reply he said that he thought it important that I should not fail to keep my engagement, but if I would consent to preach at Salem in the morning and afternoon, he would send his phaeton to Kettering for me on Sunday morning, return me to Kettering immediately after the afternoon service, and place in my hands sufficient means to pay for the hire of a gig to convey me to Deenethorpe. Accordingly, the carriage was at Salem Chapel [162] door at half past three, we reached Kettering before half past four, and found Mr. Lewis with a gig waiting at my door for me. I drank two cups of tea without sitting down, and then by economizing our time we reached our destination within two minutes of six o'clock, and found a large congregation assembled not only from Deenethorpe, but also from several surrounding villages.

While we were singing the first hymn the constable came and said, "I cannot allow you to preach here, it is the public road" (which however, was not *blocked* by us). I replied, "I will speak to you, sir, when the service is closed, if you will wait until then." He stood about ten yards from me while I read out of the fourth chapter of Acts, "Whether it be right to hearken unto you more than unto God, judge ye, etc., etc." At the close of the prayer he had withdrawn to a distance of more than a hundred yards: at the close of the service he was quite gone, and I saw him no more. [163] Preached from Acts 16.29,31.

Having concluded the service I said, "I was sorry to learn that my friends who came hither a fortnight ago were interrupted in their work, and shamefully treated. Our Master, Jesus Christ has bidden his servants to go into all the world, and preach the gospel to every creature. As Deenethorpe is in the world, we feel that we are obeying his command by coming here. The winter season is fast approaching, so that we shall probably not be able to come any more *this* year: but should we live to see the next Spring, we shall then, by the will of God visit you again. Our only object is to do good to your souls. And I wish you distinctly to understand that so often as my friends are interrupted here, I shall, if alive and well, preach here on the next Sabbath."

When the friends went in the following March, they had scarcely reached the village ere a man said to them, "You said Bingley would be met with, and he has been met with: [164] he has lost four horses since you were here." The next year he was discharged from his farm, the immediate [cause] being, I believe, his having offended his landlord by an infringement of the Game Laws. I have preached in Deenethorpe since this time, but there has not, to my knowledge been a vestige of disturbance since 1834.

On July 15th, 1835, I preached a sermon to a District Meeting of Sunday School teachers held at Carlton, Beds.

My friend, the Rev. John Ashby, having completed his term of study at Newport Pagnell College, became for a time pastor of the Independent church at Brackley. On his expressing a wish to spend a Lord's day with his parents at Kettering, I consented to exchange services with him on August 23rd. Having walked nearly the whole distance to Brackley (34 miles) on the Saturday, and preached thrice on Sunday, I started at six o'clock on Monday morning, [165] walked to Middleton Cheney to take breakfast with the Rev. J. Stonehouse (pastor of the Baptist Church in that village, and subsequently a highly esteemed Baptist Minister in Australia), then walked to Banbury, and from thence twenty-two miles further to Oxford. Traversed the city before returning to rest, then early the next morning visited the Botanical Garden, rambled over the delightful grounds of New College, went into some of the studies of the collegians (it being vacation they were not at Oxford), spent a considerable time in the splendid and beautiful Chapel of the College, then turned my face homeward, walking through Bicester and Buckingham to Stoney Stratford, or rather Old Stratford, which I reached in the evening, having walked every step of full seventy miles in the two days, without feeling specially wearied.

Having heard on Saturday that Northampton races were to be on Wednesday, I thought I should not like to be seen on the road from Northampton on that day, as it [166] might give rise to a report that I had been to the races. I therefore started from Stratford on a cross country journey of twenty two or twenty three miles, but alas! I had scarcely been an hour on the road ere my left knee began to fail me. In a few minutes the pain became excruciating, and continued to be so all the twenty miles to Kettering, almost every step being taken in agony, and no probability arising that I might be overtaken by a conveyance which would help me on my way. Amongst the myriads of miles I have walked, this was unquestionably the most painful day's journey I ever performed. I passed through Earl's Barton and Orlingbury, at either of which places friends would have welcomed me to a lodging, but I judged that I should not be able to walk at all on the next day, which proved to be the fact. However, though the special goodness of God I was enabled to reach home in safety, having in addition to preaching thrice on the Sunday walked nearly 130 miles in the four days, an [167] over exertion I have never attempted to repeat.

In the last week of February 1836 my very highly valued friend and father in the ministry the Rev. C. Vorley of Carlton, Beds., lost his eldest daughter by death. She wished me to preach her funeral sermon from Phil. 3.9. "And be found in him", which I did on March 1st. The audience was very large, as she was widely respected and beloved. She was truly one of the excellent of the earth, her only fault within my knowledge being her contracting a very uncongenial and unwise marriage.

The Kettering Provident Friendly Society (often called the British School Club) was formed on March 7th, 1836. I was appointed one of its auditors, and continued to be annually re-elected to that office until my removal to Oakham in 1849.

[Chartism and Temperance]
The Kettering Radical Association (afterwards known by the name of the Kettering Chartist Society) was commenced early in [168] 1836, and appointed me its Treasurer. I attended nearly all its meetings, and wrote several pamphlets in defence of its principles.[27] Those principles have from that time to this been my political creed, yet while I would urge them on the adoption of every one, I would not counsel any minister to attend political meetings so frequently as I did.

On June 12th, 1836, I preached at Oakham for the first time, little then thinking that fifteen years of my life would be spent in that town, and that four members of my own (family) would be intered in the burial ground of the chapel I then occupied. In the same year, I also preached for the first time at Rothwell, Great Easton, Steventon [Stevington] (Beds), Brigstock, etc., etc.

[169] In January & February 1837 the Influenza was very prevalent in many parts of the country. In Kettering alone more than 1500 persons suffered therefrom, but by the Lord's kindness I wholly escaped the scourge.

On Monday, October 23rd, 1837, my truly excellent friend and

---

27 Notably, *A Letter to the Rev. George Bugg, A. B., Curate of Desborough, Northamptonshire. Containing a Summary of the Principles, Objects, and Means of Radicalism. By a member of the Kettering Radical Association*, 1837, *Review of the Rev. A. Brown's Address*, and *Our Rights: or, The Just Claims of the Working Classes, stated in a letter to the Rev. T. H. Madge, Curate of Kettering, by the Kettering Radical Association*, 1839 [See Appendix 4].

father in the ministry, the Rev. Charles Vorley, exchanged earth for heaven, aged 71. He had a severe attack of Influenza in the preceding winter from which he never recovered. Indeed, in May he was reported to be dead. He had been pastor of the Baptist Church at Carlton (Beds.) nearly 44 years. He was an eminently devoted man of God. His remains were interred in the graveyard of his chapel on Friday October 27th, on which occasion I, in compliance with his request, preached his funeral sermon from words chosen by himself, Acts 7.59, "Lord Jesus, receive my spirit." Although the weather was unfavourable the audience was very large. Lady [170] Elizabeth Percival, sister to Lord Egmont and also to the Right Hon. Spencer Percival, M.P. for Northampton, who was shot by Bellingham in the lobby of the House of Commons on May 12th, 1812, was present. She was a kind-hearted and munificent friend to Mr. Vorley.

On Monday, October 30th, the Kettering Radical Association, of which I was Treasurer, had the honour to entertain Daniel Whitton Harvey, Esq, M.P. at a public dinner at the *Old White Horse* Inn. I and my brother Edward, Mr. Joseph Lea, now Baptist Minister at Weston-by-Weedon, Messrs. W. Goodman, Leatherland, Loasby, C. Wilson, Chester, etc. etc. spoke to the several toasts which were proposed. Mr. Harvey spoke thrice, his first speech occupying an hour and forty minutes. The speech of the evening, next to Mr. Harvey's, was that of our young friend William Goodman. Mr. Harvey was so pleased with it that he wished William Goodman to accept a situation in the office of the [171] *True Sun* newspaper, of which Mr. Harvey was then proprietor, but the young man could not bear the thought of leaving his widowed mother, and therefore declined the overture. It was well he did so, inasmuch as exactly a month after Mr. Harvey's visit, dear William Goodman died. When a boy, he used frequently on a winter's evening to spend an hour or more at my house for instruction. The *Kettering Magazine* for December 1837 says, "For depth of thought, soundness of judgement, force of remark, and undismayed avowal of the convictions of his mind, he has left no equal in our town, perhaps not in the county." On the day following his decease, the Kettering Radical Association unanimously resolved, "That this meeting deeply deplores the death of its highly valued member, Mr. William Goodman, woolcomber, from whose enlightened and profound acquaintance with political science this Association has derived inestimable advantages, and to whom it owes no small share of the reputation it has attained."

[172] Monday, April 2nd, 1838, will ever be memorable to me as the day on which I first saw Mrs. Jenkinson (then Miss Ashford). It needed not two sights of her to steal my heart.

On the last Lord's day in that month I complied with the request of the Baptist Church at Bilston in Staffordshire, that I would preach their Sunday school sermons. I remained there throughout the week, for the purpose of preaching there on the following Sunday. In the course of the week I preached at the Darkhouse Chapel, Cozeley, Wednesbury and Bilston. Went to Wolverhampton, Walsall, Darlaston, Willenhall and other places in the neighbourhood. Descended into a coalmine at Bilston of more than 300 feet depth. Also saw the smelting of iron, went to the top of one of the furnaces, and also into the casting shed at the time of tapping the furnace, and the letting of the smelted metal. Moreover, saw the manufacture of sheet plates of tin, also the casting of brass, etc., etc.

[173] My host, Mr. Paul Bissell, one of the deacons of the church, repeatedly pressed me to become pastor of the church, but with that overture I did not feel myself at liberty to comply.

When standing on Willenhall bridge on Thursday I had my first view of a railway train; rode for the first time in a railway carriage on the following Monday, May 7th. Only a single line of rails was then laid from Birmingham to Rugby, which was then pro temp. a terminus. It being the first Monday a train had run on that line, crowds of spectators were on the bridges at Coventry, etc., etc.

When bidding farewell to Mr. Bissell on Monday morning he said, "You will not reach home tonight, shall you?" "Yes," I replied, "if the Lord please I shall be at home by twelve o'clock." Accordingly I travelled to Birmingham by omnibus: walked a good deal about Birmingham with my cousin who lived there, reached Rugby by train at 3 p.m., went up to Rugby town, walked from thence [174] to Hillmorton, Crick, West Haddon, Coton, Hollowell, Creaton, Brixworth, Scaldwell, Old, and Cransley to Kettering. Having got out of the nearest way twice, and consequently made the journey one of more than thirty miles, in every step of which I had to carry a heavy load, I yet, by the good hand of my God upon me, had my hand on the latch of my own door, when the chimes of the church clock were playing twelve.*

I commenced the year 1839 at Rushden, very interesting prayer meetings being held in connexion with the Old Baptist Church in that village on New Year's Day. About a dozen Baptist Ministers were present. On May 22nd the Rev. G. Hall was ordained pastor of the Baptist Church at Carlton, as successor to the Rev. C. Vorley. In

---

* [Jenkinson's footnote] For a further account of this visit to Bilston, see Eleven Days Journal, "Kettering Magazine" June 1838.

compliance [175] with the request of the Church I preached in the evening.

The year 1840 was in some respects an unusually active and important one to me. I was again at Rushden on New Year's Day, to attend another series of prayer meetings about to be held there. Early in the morning of January 2nd I gave an address "On the Connexion of Christian Zeal with Christian Happiness." I shewed that earnestness, activity and benevolence each yields enjoyment to its possessor. The miser finds pleasure in counting his silver and gold, because in doing so he obeys the law of earnestness, the sportsman finds pleasure in the chase, because he therein obeys the law of activity, the philanthropist finds pleasure in acts of kindness, because he therein obeys the law of benevolence. The lack of larger measures of enjoyment in the Christian church arises from the deficiency of earnestness, activity [176] or benevolence, and too often a deficiency of all the three, etc., etc.

When the principle of Total Abstinence from intoxicating drinks was first introduced into Kettering, I was decidedly opposed to it. I wrote against it in the *Kettering Magazine* and preached against it, Text I Corinthians 10.30. I, moreover, publicly opposed one of its lecturers in the British School Room. But observing the good resulting from its efforts in our town, my hostility gradually abated until, in December 1839, I was earnestly desired to preside at a Temperance Meeting proposed to be held in a malt chamber in Swan Street. Having objected to do so on the ground that I was neither an abstainer, nor even convinced of the soundness of its fundamental principle, I was met by the reply, "We wish to have the chair occupied by a sort of middle man, and as thou art now not greatly opposed to us we think that [177] thou art just the man." On this ground I consented to comply with the request. In the course of the meeting I took occasion to point out what I deemed one or two mistakes into which the speakers had fallen. Yet, towards the close of the meeting, Mr. Thomas Cook (then of Market Harborough, but subsequently well known as the Railway Excursionist) said, "I predict that our Chairman will become a Teetotaller before this day twelvemonth." And surely enough when the next public meeting was held in Kettering (March 9th 1840) I signed the teetotal pledge, and being again chairman, I introduced Mr. Cook to the meeting as the prophet of Market Harborough, adding, that though his prediction was verified, I had, when it was made, no more expectation of ever becoming a total abstainer than I had of becoming Emperor of China.

The fact was that, on the next day after our meeting in December, I was walking to Cransley to preach there that evening, and when about halfway to that village I [178] overtook an old man who said, "Do you know, Sir, that Solomon Thompson is dead?" I replied, "No. Is he?" "Yes," he rejoined, "he was, as you know, accustomed to visit the public house. He was there last night until ten o'clock. On reaching home he found his wife was gone to bed, but according to her wont she had left some broth for him on the hob of the grate. He went to the cupboard it is thought either for salt or pepper, and finding a paper there with something of the kind in it he put it into his broth, which he then ate, in consequence of which he was speedily taken ill and died. Either he was so intoxicated that he did not [know] what he was doing, or so wretched that he intentionally took the powder (arsenic) to destroy himself." Having parted with the old man I thought, "Ah! This comes of strong drink. At the very time I was arguing against one or two insignificant errors of teetotal speakers that accursed [179] drink was suddenly plunging a soul into eternity within three miles of us!" Very likely this thought came from Heaven into my heart in answer to the prayers of some pious souls on my behalf. However that might be, my mind was from that hour decided in favour of total abstinence, though for various reasons I did not publicly avow until the meeting in March above referred to. In the interval, first one abstainer and then another, strongly pressed me to sign the temperance pledge, to whom I repeatedly replied, "I shall be a teetotaller when some of you are not," which, alas! proved but too correct an anticipation. I should probably have signed in January or February had I not foreseen that well nigh as soon as I had done so I should be called upon publicly to state my reasons for becoming an abstainer, and in other ways to take an active part in the movement. I therefore deemed it important to make [180] myself well acquainted with its principles and arguments before openly committing myself to the cause. Hence, I have never from that day to this had a moment's doubt on the question. Assuredly, it has in no way injured either my health, my character or my usefulness. About a month subsequent to my signing the pledge I was engaged to preach at Wellingborough, and being somewhat unwell I sent for, I believe, four pennyworth of brandy, and took less than half of it, as a medicine: but instead of benefiting me, it made me so much worse that some of the leading members of the church at Wellingborough said that teetotalism was certainly tending to rob the church of Christ of some of its valuable members and ministers, for they had never previously seen me look so ill. Alas! for the fallibility of human judgement! It was not teetotalism but the brandy which cause that hue of sickness. From that hour to this I have never either [181] touched or tasted a drop of any kind of alcoholic liquor, except at the Lord's table, and for several years not even there, as my friends at Kettering kindly consented to use unfermented wine at the Lord's supper.

My anticipations that I should soon be called upon to take an active part in the temperance movement speedily began to be realized.

The Midland Temperance Association (which comprised Leicestershire, Rutland, Northamptonshire, and parts of Warwickshire, Derbyshire, and Nottinghamshire) unanimously requested me to preach a total abstinence sermon at the Quarterly Meeting of delegates at Mount-sorrell [Leicestershire] on June 24th, 1840. In compliance with this request I occupied the pulpit of the Wesleyan Chapel in that town in the morning of that day, and preached from I Thessalonians 5.22 "Abstain from all appearance of evil." At the public meeting in the evening the delegates (of whom a large number were [182] present) unanimously requested me to send the sermon to the press. It having been in that for more than thirty years before the public, nothing more need be said thereupon.[28]

The first of April in that year did not pass over me without leaving a brandmark of folly on my brow, I having on that day commenced the least wise of all my many pecuniary outlays, *viz.* the erection of a large room for the accommodation of the Temperance and other societies. For a year or two the room was frequently occupied by several societies, but it proved on the whole a very unprofitable investment, save that, having on leaving Oakham, transformed the building into a dwelling-house for myself and family, I have from 1864 been enabled to live free of rent.

In the month of March I was requested to preach two sermons at the opening of the Baptist Chapel at Spratton. I earnestly endeavoured to stave off the service, [183] but at last was induced to engage to preach once, and was then almost compelled to undertake a second service. On both morning and evening the attendance and collections were far beyond the expectations of the friends of the cause. In compliance with their desire, the evening sermon was published.[29] Two thousand copies were printed, nearly all of which were speedily disposed of. Text Joshua 22.21-29. On June 16th, I preached the anniversary sermon on behalf of the Baptist Chapel at Bozeat.

My Temperance work rapidly increased. In addition to the sermon at Mountsorrell (Leicestershire) already referred to, I had to preach or lecture on its behalf at Wellingborough, Northampton, Coventry, Rushden, Leicester, etc., etc. My lecture at Rushden was productive of signal and enduring good. For ten years previous I had

28 *The Duty of Christians to Abstain from all Appearances of Evil. A Sermon Preached at the Quarterly Meeting of Delegates of the South Midland Temperance Association held at Mountsorrel, Leicestershire, June 24th 1840.*

29 *The Altar of Testimony a Copy of the Altar of Sacrifice:The substance of a sermon at the opening of the Baptist Meeting House, Spratton, Northamptonshire.* Toller Printer, Kettering, 1840, 2nd thousand.

somewhat frequently preached in that village, and lectured "On the Tides", [184] "On the advantages of knowledge", etc., but in the beginning of December 1840, my friend the Rev. J. Whittemore, pastor of the Old Baptist Church at Rushden, wrote to me to say that he was very desirous to introduce the total abstinence movement into Rushden, and that as I stood well in the estimation of the friends there, he thought none could do it so effectively as I. He said he would leave the *way* of doing it wholly to my choice. I might either deliver a temperance lecture in his chapel, or preach a temperance sermon there, or preach a sermon on any other subject, and deliver a lecture afterwards. I answered that I should be happy to come, and that I thought the last-named of the three courses suggested was the more eligible one. I said I would (D.V.) come over on Thursday December 10th.

On the evening of that day a good congregation assembled in the Chapel. At the close of the service I said I wished to speak to them for a short time, certainly no [185] more than half an hour on the Temperance question. If any did not wish to hear anything on that subject, or if any could not conveniently stay, I should be glad if they would leave before the commencement of my address, but that I should be still more glad if as many as possible would remain.

A few left, but a large number remained. I just simply stated my reasons for becoming a teetotaller, then closed without having exceeded the half hour. Left the pulpit with no expectation of hearing of any good resulting from my address. When Lo! to my surprize Mr. Whittemore came hurriedly into the vestry to me, and said "Have you the pledge book?" "No," I replied, "I did not anticipate that anyone would wish to sign the pledge." "O, write it down at once," he rejoined, "for several persons are waiting to sign it." I accordingly did so, and some who signed it that night have kept it unbroken through nearly thirty years. And although a principal landed [186] proprietor of the parish had said, "Rushden is such a notoriously drunken place that it will be of no use for anyone to try to introduce teetotalism there," the cause has advanced so decidedly and steadily that there is no village in the county in which it has made greater progress. Some who, previous to December 1840, seemed to be well nigh hopelessly ruined in health, mind, soul and circumstances, have for nearly thirty years been reclaimed and honourable characters, but some of them prosperous tradesmen. I have received from them repeated and abundant expressions of gratitude for having introduced teetotalism into their midst, but to God be all the glory.

On Lord's day, December 27th, three Temperance sermons were preached in the New Hall, Wellington Street, Leicester. That in the morning by a Primitive [187] Methodist preacher, that in the afternoon by Mr. James Teare, the popular Temperance lecturer, the one in the evening by myself. Mr. Thomas Cooper[30] the talented lecturer on the "Being of a God" and the "Evidences of Christianity", told me some years afterwards that he signed the Temperance pledge that night in consequence of hearing my sermon. Text, II Corinthians 5.10-16.

On January 18th, 1841, I spoke at a Temperance meeting at Burton Latimer, and on the following Friday and Saturday presided at Mr. Millington's temperance lectures at Kettering. Took part in a temperance meeting at Rushden on the 28th, and on the 29th presided at another lecture at Kettering by Mr. Millington. On February 4th, I delivered a temperance lecture at Kettering, and on the 11th gave a lecture at Kettering on the imprisonment of Mr. W. Baines of Leicester for non-payment of church rates. On June the 1st I gave a temperance lecture at Roade, and [188] another on the following evening in the old Town Hall, Northampton. On the 29th took part in a temperance public meeting at Wellingborough. On July 23rd I gave an address at a Sunday School tea meeting at Isham, and August 2nd addressed a temperance meeting at Rushden.

[*Jenkinson's visit to Manchester and meeting Richard Cobden*]
On August 17th and following three days I attended the Anti Corn-Law Conference of Ministers of all Denominations at Manchester. Went to Blisworth on Monday morning, from thence (accompanied by the Rev. Joseph Ashford, of Burton, and the Rev. J. Gravestock, of Old) by train to Manchester. Richard Cobden, Esq., M.P., having from his first appearance as an author been a special favourite of mine, I read the greater part of one of his works while on the journey, and was highly delighted with it.[31] Our instructions directed us to apply at Mr. Gadsby's, bookseller, for our respective billets. Thither therefore we repaired. It was betwixt nine and ten o'clock, and the railway trains from various parts of the kingdom having [189] just arrived, the large room was crowded with ministers. On my name being called a gentleman rose and said, "I shall be happy to accommodate Mr. Jenkinson at my house." I had scarcely a moment given me to wonder who the very pleasant and intelligent looking gentleman could be, ere the secretary said, "Mr. Cobden will be glad to have you as his guest, Mr. Jenkinson." I was so overpowered with delight that I could scarcely

---

30 A largely self-educated working-man, Cooper (1805-92) was a Leicester Chartist (who served two years in prison), then, after Chartism, was a Temperance activist and a lecturer on religious belief. His poem *Purgatory of Suicides; a Prison Rhyme in Ten Books* was published in 1845, and his *The Life of Thomas Cooper Written by Himself* in 1882.

31 Richard Cobden, a Manchester merchant, was the thinker and leading strategist of the Anti-Corn Law League. There is a statue to him in Manchester.

acknowledge my gratitude. Mr. Cobden almost instantly left his seat, and coming round to the side of the table at which I stood said, "Will you have the kindness to take my arm, Mr. Jenkinson?" We therefore traversed the streets arm in arm until we reached Mr. Cobden's spacious dwelling, which is, I believe, now known as Owens College.[32]

Mr. Ashford having told me that he could not take Mr. Gravestock with him, and that, on account of his extreme deafness, Mr. Gravestock did not wish to go wholly amongst strangers, when thanking Mr. Cobden before we left the billeting room, [190] I told Mr. Cobden that I had a friend with me who was nearly deaf, and who would therefore be glad to accompany me, if not inconvenient to Mr. Cobden. "O, let him come with you by all means," said Mr. Cobden.

About twelve ministers besides myself were located at his house. Amongst them were the Revs T. Spencer, B. Parsons, Ebenezer Davis, Joseph Davis, T. Crumpton, and Mr. John Brown, a *very* intelligent lay preacher from Dorsetshire. Their conversation was highly instructive. When at dinner on Wednesday Mr. Cobden said, "I should like to ask you gentlemen whether you take the *Nonconformist* newspaper. I am on principle a Churchman, but I gave ten pounds towards the establishment of that paper, and I think it so clearly brings out your principles that in my view if you do not take that paper, you ought to." Having been a subscriber to the *Nonconformist* from its commencement, I was of course very pleased with this remark.

[191] Our accommodation was, of course, first rate. Yet on Wednesday night my bedfellow, Mr. Gravestock, said to me, "This is a poor house, Br. Jenkinson." I thought it so much the reverse that I could not even imagine in what respect it could be deemed a *poor* house, and therefore asked, "Why, what in the world do you mean?" "Oh it is a *very* poor house," reiterated Mr. Gravestock "Why so?" I inquired. "No smoking allowed here," he rejoined. I must confess I had never thought of *that*, inasmuch as not being a smoker, I had not felt the privation. But poor Gravestock felt it so much that on the next morning he left Manchester, and took his journey homewards.

The business of the Conference commenced at ten o'clock on Tuesday morning, and at the very outset there seemed to be a likelihood of a fracas. On a motion being made for the appointment of a preliminary chairman, the always outspoken but eccentric [192] Rev. William Gadsby, who gloried in being the Antinomian Baptist Minister

---

32 Owens College was the foundation from which the modern University of Manchester developed.

of Manchester, arose from his seat, and in a stentorian voice which almost startled the Conference cried out, "It is a shame. Seven hundred ministers gathered together for the discussion of a very important matter, and not to ask the Lord's guidance and blessing on their deliberations! I say it is a shame." The Rev. D. Nolan replied, "The question whether or not the conference should be opened with prayer, had been considered by the Committee and was at that moment being re-considered. If the conference will exercise forbearance for a few minutes the final decision of the Committee on the question will be presented." The Rev. Dr. Massie said, "One source of the difficulty of deciding this question is that the conference includes several Roman Catholic clergymen, none of whom can conscientiously take part in any other religious service than [193] their own. Consequently to open each day's business with prayer would exclude them from that part of the proceedings, and perhaps thus tend to weaken their attachment to the cause we have met to promote."

After the lapse of a few minutes the Provisional Committee reported that having maturely deliberated on the question they were quite agreed in their desire, on the one hand, not even to appear to ignore the importance of prayer for the divine blessing on the proceedings of the conference, nor on the other to imperil its unanimity by intermingling any religious service therewith. They had therefore to announce that the business of the conference would commence on each morning at ten o'clock, and that a prayer meeting to implore the blessing of God on its deliberations would be held each morning at nine o'clock, in Oak Street Baptist Chapel, which was near at hand. This truly wise recommendation was accordingly acted upon, and the unanimity [194] of the conference thereby preserved.

The four days on which the conference was held were amongst the finest ever known in Manchester, which from its situation betwixt the sea and the Derbyshire hills, is visited with a share of wet weather beyond that of most other places. When at supper on Friday, Mr. Cobden in expressing his gratitude for the fineness of the week said, "A Frenchman spent two or three weeks in Manchester on business, during which it rained heavily every day. About seven years afterwards a gentleman of Manchester called on the Frenchman in Paris, when one of the first questions asked by Monsieur was, 'Has it stopped raining at Manchester yet?'" After the close of the conference on Friday a public tea was provided at one shilling each in the Corn Exchange, which was crowded to excess, and a very numerously attended public meeting was held in the [195] evening in the large Free Trade Hall. Although the *Times* and some other papers unsparingly ridiculed the Conference, and even descended so low as to assert that "the Jewish 'old clo' stalls in

Rag Fair had been ransacked for black coats for the ministers delegated to the Conference," it is impossible to question that the proceedings of that week exerted a very material influence in hastening the repeal of the Corn Laws.

The Rev. Thos. Spencer, perpetual curate of Hinton Charterhouse, near Bath, was the only [Anglican] clergyman present and the Rev. J. Nelson, of Birmingham, the only Wesleyan Methodist.

I returned home on Saturday by way of Leeds, and from thence to Leicester, from which latter town I intended to walk to Kettering, but was favoured with a ride for three or four miles. Preached three sermons on Sunday in reference to the Conference. Texts Ezek. 2.9,10, Psalms 115.16, Acts [196] 15.6. On August 31st, a large public meeting was held in the British Schoolroom to afford the Rev. William Robinson[33] and myself to present our Reports of the Conference. The building was so full that more than a hundred persons failed to gain admittance.

On Tuesday, September 21st, I preached the anniversary sermon for the Primitive Methodists of Wellingborough. Their Chapel was filled on the occasion. Gave a Temperance lecture at Kettering on the 23rd, preached a harvest thanksgiving sermon at Ringstead on the 27th, gave a Temperance lecture at Blunham (Beds) on the 29th, a harvest thanksgiving address at Sandy [Beds.] on the afternoon of the 30th, and a Temperance lecture there in the evening.

Lady Gertrude Fitzpatrick of Farming Woods having died in the beginning of October, and I having preached at Brigstock Independent Chapel somewhat frequently, I was requested to preach a sermon there in reference to her death. I did so on [197] October 10th. The chapel was crowded to excess. Text, Proverbs 31.31. Within a little more than nine weeks afterwards her Ladyship's sister (when living they were invariably seen together), Lady Ann Fitzpatrick, also died. Another communication was therefore forwarded to me, which stated that as my sermon in October had given such universal satisfaction they should be greatly obliged if I would preach a sermon in reference to Lady Ann's death. I therefore did so on the evening of December 19th. The chapel was again thronged. Text II Sam. 1.23.

On October 25th took part in a missionary meeting at Isham. On December 8th, delivered a Temperance lecture at Market Harborough.

---

33 William Robinson was J. K. Hall's successor as minister of Little Meeting (from 1829 to 1852). He had his theological differences with Jenkinson, but on religious and party politics they were both Radicals.

On January 30th, 1842 I preached for the first time at Olney [Bucks.]. On March 8th [illeg.] gave two Temperance lectures at Oundle. On April 17th preached a funeral sermon at Ringstead for the Rev. J. L. Abington, pastor of the Baptist Church in that village. Text, John 6.37.

[198] On January 4th, 1842, a Tent of the Independent Order of Rechabites,[34] whose headquarters have always been at Manchester, was opened at Kettering, and also a Tent of Female Order of Rechabites, whose headquarters were at South Shields. I was unanimously chosen Secretary to both Tents, and continued to hold the office until my removal to Oakham.

On March 31st a public meeting was held in Kettering for the purpose of electing a delegate to the Complete Suffrage Conference appointed to be held at Birmingham on April 5th, and following days. I was unanimously elected, and accordingly went to Birmingham on Monday April 4th. I attended all the meetings of the conference. The excellent Joseph Sturge was elected chairman. Messrs. John Bright (now M.P.) E. Parry, barrister, (now Serjeant Parry) Edward Miall, Rev. A. S. Wade, D.D. (vicar of St Nicholas, Warwick), Rev. J. P. Mursell (Leicester) Henry Vincent, William Lovett, John Collins, etc. were some of the 84 members of the conference.[35] On Thursday Mr. Sturge invited eight or nine of us to dine with him, we therefore had the pleasure of visiting his neat [199] and beautiful house and grounds at Edgbaston. On the following Thursday a large public meeting was held at Kettering in the British School Room (the Rev. W. Robinson, chairman) for the purposes of receiving my report of the proceedings of the Conference. I addressed the meeting for an hour and a half. Persons of widely different political views were present, yet the cordial thanks of the meeting were unanimously given to me for my services in attending the conference, and for the honest and satisfactory report I had presented.

[1842: Baptist Missionary Society celebrations in Kettering]
The Jubilee of the Baptist Missionary Society being appointed to be held at Kettering at the end of May, the Committee of the Midland Temperance Society advised the members of the Kettering branch to prepare an address pressing the principles of total abstinence on the

---

34 The Ancient Order of Rechabites, founded in 1835, was a Friendly Society for Temperance people. Claiming to follow the tribe of Rechab in the Old Testament who foreswore the juice of the grape and dwelt in the desert, Rechabite branches were called "Tents". Uniquely for that time they recruited women as well as men.

35 As this list of names shows, Complete Suffrage was an early attempt to form a Reform alliance from Anti-Corn Law League people (e.g. Bright), Nonconformists (e.g. Miall, Mursell and Jenkinson) and Chartists (Vincent, Lovett, Collins). It failed. It was not until twenty years later that these groups finally came together in Gladstone's Liberal Party.

attention and adoption of the ministers and visitors who were expected, and, contrary to my wishes, urged me to write it, to which at length I consented.[36]

On Sunday evening, May 29th, I preached a sermon in Ebenezer Chapel, in reference to the approaching jubilee. Text Lev. 25.8-12. The public services continued in [200] Fuller chapel on Tuesday evening. Prayer was offered by the Rev. J. Hoby, D.D., after which the Rev. B. Godwin, D.D., preached an admirable sermon from Psalms 126.3. The chapel not being large enough to accommodate all who wished to be present, another service was held at the same time in the Independent Chapel: sermon by the Rev. A. Leslie. On Wednesday morning at half past six a large prayer meeting was held in Fuller Chapel, Mr. Grozer, editor of the *Baptist Magazine* read and prayed, and the Rev. C. Stovel delivered an address. At half past ten the immense tent which had been erected in the grounds of the Mission House was thronged with an attentive audience. Prayer was offered by the Rev. Dr. Acworth, and the Rev. E. Steane, D.D., preached from Isaiah 11.31. The sermon occupied nearly two hours in its delivery (an hour too much). In its midst the preacher sat down and sucked an orange. I held one of the large plates at the collection, and it was truly well weighted, chiefly with silver, but also with a considerable number of gold pieces. Many hundreds of persons [201] being unable to obtain admittance into the tent or grounds, another service was held at the same time in the Independent Chapel, sermon by the Rev. W. Brock. Text I Cor. 3.21-23. After a concert of sacred music at Fuller Chapel in the afternoon, a public meeting was held in the tent, which was addressed by W. B. Gurney Esq, chairman, Dr. Cox, J. Tritton, Esq, Revs. A.G. Fuller, J. P. Mursell, W. Brock, W. Knibb and J. Tinson. At the same time, other meetings were held in Fuller Chapel and the Independent Chapel. At eight o'clock on Thursday morning, another public meeting was held in the tent, and another in the British School room on Friday afternoon. About twelve thousand strangers were believed to be in Kettering during the Jubilee. At the formation of the Society in 1792 the sum collected was £13 2s.6d. The Jubilee Committee desired that the total collections in 1842 should be a hundredfold greater. In this they fully succeeded, the sum realized being above £1,300. I had about 150 persons at my house on the occasion: some of them to breakfast, some to luncheon, some to dinner, some to tea, some to supper, some [202] to sleep, some to all, and some to neither.

On June 23rd, I gave an Address to a Complete Suffrage Meeting

---

36 *The Duty of Christians to Abstain from all Appearances of Evil. A Sermon presented at the Quarterly meeting of delegates of the South Midland Temperance Association held at Mountsorrel, Leicestershire, June 24th 1840.*

at Kettering, on the 29th addressed a Temperance Tea meeting at Northampton, on the 30th delivered a Lecture in that town on Rechabitism, and repeated that lecture at Daventry on July 27th.

Sir Arthur de Capell Brooke, Bart., of Great Oakley, having on August 9th provided tea and cake for the teetotallers of Cottingham & Middleton, and any friends they thought proper to invite, I, with several others of Kettering, attended and addressed the meeting. I also took part in the Baptist Jubilee Missionary meeting at Thrapston on September 26th, on which occasion the Rev. J. Aldis, of London, delivered one of the most splendid speeches I ever heard.

The Baptist Missionary Society, having on October 2nd completed its fifty years, I on the evening of that day preached a sermon in reference thereto from Matt. 21.42. In the same week I attended the Rechabite district meeting at Buckingham. In going thither I managed to have three breakfasts on one morning. My sister-in-law said I had better take breakfast before leaving [203] home. I accordingly did so at half past one o'clock. Then had a very dark walk to Wellingborough, from which Mr. Dunmar, our Treasurer, said he should start with a gig betwixt four and five. I reached his house soon after four, and one of the first words he said to me was, "You are just right for breakfast: we are just going to begin." I therefore took a second breakfast. On arriving at Newport Pagnell a little before eight, and calling on a Quaker there, he said "I am glad to see thee, Friend Dunmar, thou and thy friend are just in time for breakfast." Thus I had a third breakfast: though in reality neither was literally a *break fast*. Returned home by way of Northampton. Went forthwith to the Baptist Mission Jubilee Bazaar then being held at the *George* Inn in that town. I knew that Miss Ashford (see page 172) had beautifully painted two speel cups for that bazaar. My fear was that they would be sold before my arrival: but on entering the room I instantly and gladly saw them, and presently made them mine. Had the price been five times as much as was asked I would [204] cheerfully have given it.

Gave a Rechabite lecture at Oundle on November 7th. Northamptonshire being constituted a distinct Rechabite District in December, I was appointed District Secretary to the Male Tents and also to the Female Tents.

[Financial matters at Ebenezer]
In our religious movement the pressure of our chapel debt was our heaviest burden. Of course, I received no salary during the nineteen years in which that debt was being paid: though a new year's gift was annually collected for me. The erection and furnishing of the chapel had

cost nearly £500, of which sum we had borrowed £350, at five *per cent*. My people were nearly all poor, many of them *very* poor. Our largest pecuniary contributor was Mr. Philip Curtis, who in 1830 removed from Kettering to Bedworth in Warwickshire. Some of my friends were deeply concerned on that occasion, and began to fear that his leaving the town would involve us in inextricable pecuniary [205] difficulties. His removal did certainly *appear* to be an irreparable loss, and yet so far from proving so in reality, it is not too much to say that it caused our debt to be paid many years earlier than it would have been had he remained in Kettering. During the more than six years in which he had managed our financial affairs (six years in which our chapel was regularly filled with worshippers and all hearts were warm and all hands opened to the utmost of their power) only £20 of the £350 we had borrowed was repaid! He discharged the duties of the deacon's office with unimpeachable honour and honesty, but did not economize our funds so carefully as he might have done. Yet, for some little time subsequent to his removal, we financially receded instead of advancing, in so much that our weekly subscriptions towards the reduction of our debt began to be required for the payment of the interest. Under these circumstances I made the [206] following singular proposal to our remaining deacons: "If you will from the pew rents pay me sixteen pounds a year, I will engage to pay the entire principal and interest of our debt in twenty years, if Providence spares my life and continues my health so long." This was in February 1831, at which time the yearly interest we had to pay was £16.10s.0d. Consequently the deacons, though acquiescing in my proposal, thought my engagement a wild one which could not possibly be realized. Yet realized it was, in less than *twelve* years, instead of *twenty*. Of course, I intended to contribute, and did contribute, in common with my people, but I saw at the outset that my contributions would not need to be very onerous.

A circumstance which at first seemed likely to augment our pecuniary difficulties was the immediate cause of my proposal and of the steady reduction of our debt, that circumstance being that £150 of the [207] money owing was unexpectedly called in. As we were unable at once to comply with the demand I told the lender (who I knew did not need the money) that if he would have the kindness not to press us, I would in every year, on the day on which the interest was due, pay the year's interest and also £25 of the principal. This promise I strictly and literally fulfilled, the day having in no instance closed without the promised amount being paid. This, of course, reduced our total yearly interest to less than £16 after the first year: and moreover the interest continued to decrease every year, as I had foreseen it would. Having cleared off the £150, I then promised to our creditors (J. C. Gotch Esq., whose bond gave us the *right* to pay the debt by instalments) that I would in every year on the day the interest was due pay not only that but also £30 of the principal. This promise also I strictly fulfilled, nay exceeded: for when we had reduced the [208] debt to £120, I told my people that I felt certain we could as a final effort pay that off in one year, which we did: and having done so had a day of hearty gladness and thanksgiving. That memorable day was Wednesday February 15th, 1843, in the afternoon of which I preached from Lam. 2.16 "This is the day that we looked for."

I have stated these proceeding thus minutely for the instruction and encouragement of other churches who may be burdened with a heavy debt. They can scarcely be poorer than we, and it is next to impossible for them to receive a smaller amount of help from other churches than we did: for I believe the whole amount contributed by other hands than our own was less than £20. It ought, however, to be recorded that some of the members of the first Baptist Church in Kettering regularly helped us in our efforts: indeed both our creditors were leading members of that Church.

Though I have neither received nor [209] solicited aid from the Baptist Building Fund, I cannot refrain from commending it to the support of all well-wishers to the Baptist Denomination into whose hands these pages may fall. Both its object and its *modus operandi* are alike commendable. My view is that those who build a place of worship ought to consider themselves under an obligation of pay for it. On this ground, I felt myself morally required to continue at Kettering until our chapel debt was discharged. Nevertheless to a poor church, and even to some which are not *very* poor, the having to pay simultaneously interest and instalments of the principal is heavily burdensome. Having through a succession of years had to sustain such a burden I can duly appreciate the advantage of obtaining a loan free of interest, ten *per cent* of the loan being required to be repaid every year, which of course in ten years cancels the debt.

[210] Three months after the payment of our debt, the church of which I was pastor applied for admission into the Northamptonshire Baptist Association, but its application was rejected. I have subsequently learnt that the cause of our rejection was not in ourselves, but elsewhere [see Appendix 1].

[Marriage]
I have now to record the most important temporal event which has befallen me. My marriage. The love cord which my dear Miss Ashford had thrown around my heart when I first beheld her having continually become stronger and tighter our two drops were sweetly

and irresistibly drawn into one in the Superintendent's Registry Office at Northampton, July 4th, 1843. The Rev. Joseph Ashford and Mrs. Ashford were present at the ceremony, immediately after which we all travelled together in a double seated hackney coach to the Baptist Chapel at Harpole (where Mr. Ashford. was then pastor). He there gave us [211] a very suitable address and offered earnest prayers on our behalf. A goodly number of persons were present. As soon as we had dined we all travelled in the same coach to Weedon Station: where we parted from our dear parents, and took our places in the railway train for London, which by the kind providence of God we safely reached. We spent a fortnight in visiting a large number of public places in London and its vicinity: St Paul's, the British Museum, the Polytechnic, the Zoological Gardens, Madame Tussaud's, sat in the Coronation Chair in Westminster Abbey, and also on the throne in the House of Lords, went by water to Hampton Court and also to Greenwich, etc. etc. etc. On one or other of the Sundays we spent in town, we had the pleasure of hearing the Revs. T. Binney, J. Aldis, Alexander Fletcher, Dr. Allcott, etc., etc.

The annual meetings of the Independent Order of Rechabites, to which the Northampton District had appointed me its delegate, [212] commenced on Tuesday July 18th, and were continued from day to day until the evening of the 26th.

[Church and Nonconformist battles]

My happy honeymoon was, however, dashed with a drop of bitterness. On June 17th, several persons in Kettering had their goods seized and sold for non-payment of church rates. Not being then a householder I, of course, escaped the seizure, but like hundreds of others I attended the sale, and while there a nearly intoxicated police-man passing by me I very gently put my finger on his shoulder, without either intending or suspecting harm said, "Mr. B. are you not ashamed of yourself?", which all the police evidently were. After pondering over the matter for nearly a month, the leading persons connected with our parish church prompted this policeman to take out a summons against me for an assault: which summons was forwarded to me in London by post, and therefore not legally. On reaching Kettering on July 28th, I had not walked twenty yards along the street ere I was informed [213] that I should have to appear before the magistrates on Monday, August 7th. Before the arrival of that day, however, the superintendent of police called on me to say that they should abandon the summons. To which I replied, "I do not thank you for it, as I am sure the magistrates would have deemed your charge against me so frivolous and ridiculous that they would have instantly dismissed it."

The whole of this year (1843) was to be a busy one. In addition to my very frequent preaching in Kettering and other places I published a pamphlet entitled *Ebenezer*, on the occasion of the clearing our chapel from debt.[37] Also two articles for the *Children's Temperance Magazine*, one entitled "Fitness", the other, "You had better not". Also a solemn one entitled "'A Voice from the Grave', occasioned by the death of W. Mawby through strong drink" [which was] Inserted in the *Temperance Messenger* for May 1843.

A member of my church who lived at Isham, having lost his child by death, the [214] rector refused to inter it because it had not been baptized. His father therefore requested me to officiate on the occasion. Although I had done so once or twice previously in that village, having in one case given out a hymn to be sung while standing at the grave, I knew it would not be legally safe to do so under the present incumbent. Nevertheless I promised to attend. On reaching the house on Thursday, November 9th, I was forthwith informed that the rector, the two churchwardens, the parish constable, the parish clerk, and a large number of farmers and others would be in the churchyard with a view to prosecute me if I desecrated the sacred enclosure: but added the father, "Nathan Palmer's orchard adjoins the churchyard, and he is quite willing you should stand there to speak." I accordingly walked before the corpse to the churchyard gate, and there left the bearers and mourners to proceed to the grave whilst I went round to the orchard, which alas! [215] on reaching I found to be three or four feet lower than the churchyard: but a short ladder of about ten feet long stood against a stubble rick close at hand. By its aid I instantly mounted the wall, but had scarcely done so ere the rector sternly called out, "I can't allow you to stand there Mr. Jenkinson, that is consecrated ground." My father-in-law, the Rev. J. Ashford providentially was with me, and on hearing the rector's admonishment to me said, "You had better not stand there to speak." The common people knew him, but as his canonical attire was hidden by his greatcoat and he had a somewhat elegant stick in his hand, both he and I instantly perceived that the rector and other officials, and the farmers and tradesmen who had gathered in the graveyard, believed him to be my solicitor under whose guidance I was acting. On turning my eyes I noticed that about a good wheelbarrow full of stubble had fortunately been removed from the top of the rick, I therefore promptly descended from the wall, placed the [216] ladder against the rick, and found its top to be one of the best platforms it has ever been my lot to occupy, then looking down to Mr. Ashford, I said, "I believe I am quite safe here." "Yes," said he, "you are perfectly safe

---

37 *Ebenezer; or a Memorial of the Divine Goodness: addressed to the Church and Congregation Assembling in Ebenezer Baptist Chapel, Kettering on the Completion of their efforts for the Liquidation of the Debt incurred in the Erection of their Place of Worship,* 1843.

there Mr. Jenkinson." After singing a hymn I delivered an address in which I certainly did not spare to point out the egregious error, the gross inconsistency, and the demoralising tendency of the Episcopalian clergy committing the bodies of drunkards, liars, thieves, fornicators, and Sabbath breakers to the grave "in sure and certain hope of the resurrection to eternal life," and refusing to officiate at the interment of a babe who had never personally sinned, and for no stronger reason than that a little water had not been sprinkled on its face, which omission it would be hard to shew to be a sin at all, and, if a sin, it was assuredly not that of the infant. After exhorting all, whether young or old, churchmen or dissenters to see above all things that they were [217] prepared to die, I concluded with prayers, the clergyman and his abettors staying until the close of the service.

I have omitted to say that on Sunday August 20th, of this year 1843, I baptized three persons in the brook at Geddington, they having requested to be baptized *there*. I preached on the Cross [The Eleanor Cross in Geddington village] previous to the baptizing. Had a thousand persons present, some of them from distant villages, many from Kettering. During the baptism the long bridge which spans the stream was thronged with spectators. The vicar postponed commencing service in the parish church until we had concluded: the reason being, I was told, that there was no one but himself and the parish clerk within the sacred edifice.

I officiated at the opening of a female Rechabite Tent at Daventry on January 2nd 1843, gave a Temperance Lecture at Wellingborough on the 9th, at Guilsborough on the 10th, at Bedford on May 3rd, at Rugby on the 15th, at Naseby on June 12th, at Northampton on August 2nd, addressed the South [218] Midland Temperance Association at its annual meeting at Kettering on September 26th, and gave a Temperance lecture at Cubbington, near Leamington on December 25th. The secretary of the flourishing Temperance Society in that village instructed me to come to Rugby by rail, and thence by the Leamington Coach to Cubbington. I wrote specially to enquire if the coach would certainly run on Christmas Day. He replied, "It would." I therefore left Kettering soon after one o'clock in the morning, walked nineteen miles to Blisworth, (at that time our nearest railway station), having taken breakfast at Northampton: was quite in time for the train. Reached Rugby in safety, asked if the Leamington Coach was in, was told it was not, but would soon be so. Enquired of several porters and others if they were *certain* it would come on that day: to which they all replied, "Yes." However, its usual time one o'clock was past, and also two o'clock, but no coach arrived. At last one of the railway officials said, "It is not coming today, the coachman told me yesterday he [219] should not come." There was I, fifteen miles from my destination, in the afternoon of one of the shortest days, after having walked nineteen miles that morning. I therefore stated the case to the Station Master, and asked what I had better do. "You must go on to Coventry by the next train." "Thank you, and what then?" "Go by the Warwick coach." "Are you sure *that* will be here today?" "Certain," he replied. Accordingly to Coventry I went. The Warwick coach was there just ready to start. "Do you go through Cubbington?" I asked. "No," said the coachman, "but we go very near it. You will only have one or two fields to cross when you leave the coach." I feared it would be night ere I alighted, and that I should have to ramble about those unknown fields in the dark. But we passed through the far famed Kenilworth, and reached the near neighbourhood of Cubbington before the light was gone. I therefore readily crossed the fields, and on entering the village met a teetotal baker whom I had known at Wellingborough. "Oh," said he, "I knew [220] I was right. Our teetotal folk here have been fretting all day, because the coach did not run today, and therefore you could not come." "Nonsense," I said, "he is not the man to disappoint you. If they sent him down anywhere within twenty miles of Cubbington he will walk that distance, and be here in time to lecture, if not in time for tea. And here you are half an hour before tea is ready. Well I am heartily glad to see you." And a capital tea meeting we had, and a large meeting at the lecture. Several of the friends accompanied me to the cross roads on the following morning, the Leamington coach did not disappoint me on that day, I reached Rugby in safety, thence by train to Weedon, and walked from thence to Harpole, where Mrs. Jenkinson was paying a Christmas visit to our dear father and mother.

In the course of this year I took an active, and for a considerable time, a successful, [221] part in preventing a church rate being granted to the Kettering Churchwardens.

In April 1844 we held a series of special prayer meetings in our Chapel. On April 1st, for Missions at home and abroad, April 2nd, for Enquirers in our congregation, April 3rd, for the church and congregation, April 4th for Backsliders, April 5th, for our Sunday school, April 6th, for our town and the villages around. I delivered an address on the subject at each meeting.

In the same month my people appointed me their delegate to the Anti-State Church Conference about to be held in London. On April 16th I took part in the meeting held in the Independent Schoolroom for the purpose of electing the Rev. W. Robinson and Mr. J. Spence as delegates from the town to the above named conference. I reached London on the 29th. Attended the Conference prayer meeting in Eagle

Street Baptist Chapel on Tuesday morning, April 30th. Proceeded direct from thence to the *Crown & Anchor* where the Conference was opened at eleven o'clock, Rev. J. Burnet of Camberwell, Chairman. At the evening meeting the Rev. Dr. Marshall of Kirkintilloch, near [222] Glasgow, presided: on Wednesday and Thursday the Rev. Dr. Young, of Perth, the Rev. Dr. Acworth, of Yorkshire, and John Dunlop, Esq. of Edinburgh were Chairmen. At this conference the Anti-State Church Society (now the Liberation Society) was formed. On May 7th a public meeting was held in the Independent Chapel, Kettering to which I and the other delegates presented our report of the Conference. On May 27th I addressed a special meeting of the Kettering Provident Friendly Society (see p.167). On June 6th my first born child, my dear Emily, was born. The essay on the birth of a child, which I wrote at the birth of my first niece (Caroline), and which may be seen in the *Baptist Magazine* for, I believe, 1830, is still more expressive of my feelings in reference to the birth of my own child. On June 4th, T. S. Woolley, Esq. of Cottingham (Notts.) was married to Maria, third daughter of Henry Lamb, Esq. of Kettering and at the same time and place (Kettering Parish Church) Mr. J. Woolley, Esq. of Loughborough, was married to Harriett Ann, second daughter of Mr. Lamb: on which occasion I instantly [223] wrote the following stanza.

> If fitness is surely the pathway to bliss
> These ladies may look for it fully,
> For what in the world can be fitter than this,
> That Lambs should in June become Woolley?

On Wednesday July 3rd, I preached two sermons at Thurleigh, Beds, on behalf of the Baptist Chapel there, which had been lately restored. On July 28th, preached the Sunday School sermons at Stanwick, and addressed the children on the following day. Preached at Rushden on the 30th. On August 8th addressed a Sunday school tea meeting at Geddington. On September 5th, addressed a tea meeting in the British School. Preached at Risely [Beds] on the 25th, gave the charge to the Rev. Reuben Turner at his ordination as pastor of the Baptist Church, Bythorn, on the 26th. Motto, "Looking into Jesus". Preached in Salem Chapel, Wellingborough on October 6th, the afternoon sermon having special reference to the Jubilee of the London Missionary Society. Text Leviticus 25.8-12. On December 9th, addressed an Anti-Oath taking meeting at Geddington.

[224] On Tuesday November 12th, her Majesty, with Prince Albert and suite passed through Kettering on their way to visit the Marquis of Exeter [at Burghley]. Of course, our Sunday school assembled to welcome her. I and Mrs. Jenkinson obtained a very eligible

situation for seeing the whole of the royal carriages and their occupants. We had, however, previously seen the Queen when riding with Lady Gainsborough in Hyde Park in July 1843.

The following are some of my Temperance engagements in the year. January 4th, Address to the Male and Female Rechabite Tents at Kettering, January 23rd, Lecture on Rechabitism at Wellingborough, August 21st, ditto at Warwick, etc., etc.

On December 17th of this year, my next door neighbour, Mr. Richard Neal, fell asleep in Christ, aged 87. He was a *very* eccentric man, but a true Christian. As Executor to my uncle and master, Mr. William Stafford, he acted a truly upright part.

A somewhat long letter of mine on the Corn Laws was inserted in the [225] *Northampton Mercury* in April 1845. In the summer of this year I engaged in a Temperance controversy in the *Citizen* with *Veritas*, (the Rev. A. Burdett, pastor of the Baptist Church at Long Buckby). My closing letter, though approved by the editor, did not obtain insertion. It may be seen in the *Kettering Magazine* for October 1845.

On June 24th I preached the anniversary sermons at Hail Weston, Hunts. On July 2nd, delivered one of the addresses at the opening of the Baptist Chapel, Desborough, and on the following Sunday (July 6th) preached two sermons therein, and had collections towards the Chapel Fund. On September 2nd delivered one of the addresses at the recognition of the Rev. T. Lord as pastor of the Independent Church at Brigstock. On the 23rd took part in the Rechabite Festival, at Rushden; on the 30th, spoke at Temperance Tea Meeting at Brigstock. On October 7th preached two sermons at the anniversary of the Baptist Chapel at Keysoe, Beds. On December 21st, my second child, my dear and now sainted Laura, was born.[38]

[226] On Feb 16th, 17th, 1846, I gave two Temperance lectures at Spalding, Lincs. On May 1st I was summoned to appear before the magistrates for non-payment of Church rates. The Committee of the Anti-State Church Association in London having elected me as a member of its Council I attended the meeting of the Council at Leicester on May 7th, 8th and 9th. On May 6th, gave a Temperance Lecture at Higham Ferrers. On July 23rd I attended the ordination of the Rev. T. Thomas as pastor of the Independent church at Salem Chapel, Wellingborough. After dining at the *White Hart* Inn, the Rev. Thomas Toller, proposed the health of the Rev. Dr. John Pye Smith in a brief but

---

38 Laura Jenkinson died in 1868 at the age of 22.

eulogistic address. The motion was carried by acclamation. The worthy Doctor in acknowledging the vote stated the grounds of his preference of such a mode of respect to the usual one of drinking healths, and then entered at large into the reasons which led him to become a total abstainer from intoxicating drinks. During this address, which lasted about 40 minutes, the glasses filled with wine and [227] brandy stood upon the table untouched, the would-be drinkers being in as complete a fix as it is possible to imagine.

From August 19th to the 22nd I attended the annual meetings of the Independent Order of Rechabites held in New Street, Birmingham. On each night I occupied the same bedroom as the Rev. Curate of St Nicholas, Worcester, the subsequent originator and editor of *Fire Side Words* etc., etc. On Lord's day the 23rd, I preached morning and evening in Heneage Street Baptist Chapel. In the afternoon attended a prayer meeting in a dwelling house. Was astonished to hear the first women who prayed pray for me as a friend whom she had known at a distance from thence. At the close of the service I discovered that she was a member of the Rechabite Tent which I had opened at Guilsborough in January 1843.

On September 12th, 1846, I and my brother Edward and several other persons had our goods seized and sold for non-payment of Church rates. The police officers took some of my books, but I had [228] taken the precaution to place those before them which I deemed comparatively worthless. The person who thought he purchased them cheaply offered to re-sell them to me at the price he had paid for them: but I told him I was so glad to get rid of them that I would scarcely have them again as a gift. By distraining upon me, the church authorities certainly burned their fingers, as the expenses which they had to pay were several shillings more than my books were sold for. On September 23rd I preached the annual sermon at the meeting of the North Bedfordshire Sunday School Union held at Carlton.

Each number of the *Kettering Magazine* for 1847 contains a part of my poem entitled "Isabel: or the Ghost of Barton Bridge". On February 16th I gave a lecture at Wellingborough "On Water". A lady of Newport Pagnell (Bucks) being present, on returning home induced her friends to invite me to repeat it in that town, which [229] I did on April 14th. On April 5th I gave a lecture at Northampton on Rechabitism. On April 16th, Mr. Joseph Ashford (grandfather to Mrs. Jenkinson) died at Welshpool, aged 83. He was senior tenant and senior tradesman (plumber & glazier) to Earl Powis of Powis Castle. Better still, he was senior deacon of the Baptist church at Welshpool, and had uniformly used his office well.

The first Triennial Conference of the Anti-State Church Associ-ation was held in Crosby Hall, Bishopsgate Street, London on May 4th, 5th and 6th. I attended as one of the delegates from Kettering, Mr. David Townsend as delegate from Geddington. Before leaving London we visited the exhibition of paintings in the Egyptian Hall, Piccadilly, representing the Baptism of Christ: Mr. Bell, of Newcastle-on-Tyne having offered a thousand guineas for the best painting on that subject. Although the number of the paintings was I believe, about twenty, we thought none of them (not even the prize one) at all worthy of the subject. The artists would have better succeeded [230] had they taken the trouble to witness the administration of baptism in any Baptist Chapel.

On May 24th I gave a Temperance Lecture at Buckingham. On June 3rd addressed a Tea Meeting at Rothwell: on July 7th took part in the Rechabite Festival at Kettering, and on September 28th was one of the speakers at the Jubilee of the Independent Chapel at Brigstock.

On February 24th, 1848, a public meeting was held in the Independent Chapel Kettering in reference to the increasing national expenditure, and the proposal to call out the militia. I took part in the meeting. On March 7th, the Delegates who had been sent from Kettering to attend the Anti-War Conference in London, made their report to a public meeting. I and others spoke on the occasion.

The ratepayers of Kettering having resolved to extend £600 or £700 in endeavouring to obtain an Act of Parliament to compel owners of Cottages in the town to pay the rates in the stead of their tenants, I and Mr. Francis [231] one of my deacons were sent to London to oppose its passage through the Committee of the House of Commons. No one expected that we should defeat the Bill, but it was thought well that our case should be fairly presented. The favourers of the Bill in Kettering said we should not be allowed to open our lips in the Committee Room, and one or two parliamentary agents whom we saw in London thought so too. Nevertheless we went, and were received by the Committee with the greatest courtesy. I was allowed to examine Mr. Taylor as a witness for more than half an hour, and then to address the Committee for nearly another hour.[39]

On April 12th, 13th, and 14th two hundred teetotal ministers met as a Temperance Conference at Manchester. I was sent as the

---

39 Jenkinson published a pamphlet against the proposed Act in 1847, *The Injustices of Requiring Cottage Owners to pay Poor-Rates for their Tenants*. The following year, under the pseudonym "A Rate-payer" he composed a handbill *Thirty-One Reasons for Objecting to the Kettering Small tenements Rating Act* [See Appendix 6].

delegate from Northamptonshire. On Friday evening I told the lady at whose house I lodged that I should have to leave before six o'clock the next morning, but that I would not trouble her servant to rise and prepare my breakfast, as I could easily procure it at Crewe, where I believe we should have to [232] wait about half an hour for the arrival of the train from Chester, when lo! on reaching Crewe we found the Chester train waiting for us. We therefore pushed on all the way to Blisworth, and there the train for Northampton was just starting. On arriving at Northampton I thought it desirable to inquire at what time the Kettering carrier would start, and *then* get some refreshment. On reaching Abington Street I saw him, and said "How long shall you be before you leave?" "I am leaving this very minute," said he, "jump in." On entering my house after nine o'clock Mrs. J said, "Well my dear, how are you?" "Very well, thank you," I replied, "only I want my breakfast." For I had been on the move nearly sixteen hours, without an atom to eat or drink, except a halfpenny cake which I purchased after having entered the carrier's van at Northampton. I preached three sermons the next day, without any ill-effect, one being a funeral sermon for a very excellent member of my church (Joseph Tebbutt of Great Oakley,) whose employer [233] once spoke of him to me as the best man in Oakley.

On Wednesday evening May 31st, my dear son Joseph Ashford Jenkinson was born.

The churchwardens of Kettering having on June 22nd, called a parish vestry for the purpose of laying another church rate, I moved that the vestry be adjourned to July 27th, which being seconded by Mr. Taylor, and supported by the Rev. William Robinson was carried by a majority. On the arrival of that, Mr. Robinson being unavoidably from home, the task of speaking against the rate devolved on me. On a poll being demanded and taken, the rector, the Rev. Thomas H. Madge, refused to receive the votes of cottage tenants, assigning as his reason that the Kettering Small Tenements Act which had just received the royal assent had taken them out of the list of ratepayers. In opposition to this dictum I contended that how valid soever that reason might be thereafter, it had no force on that occasion, inasmuch as the vestry in connexion with which the poll was being taken [234] was not a *new* vestry but a continuance of the one commenced on June 22nd, before the Kettering Small Tenements Act had even passed the House of Lords. Excluding the cottage tenants the rate was carried, including them it was decidedly lost. Nearly twelvemonths elapsed ere the point was legally and finally decided. In March of the next year I and thirteen others were summoned for not paying the rate. We engaged Mr. Richardson, a solicitor of Leeds, to conduct our defence before the magistrates. Having heard him, the Chairman, (the Rev. J. Wetherall, of

Rushden) said, "We as magistrates do not wish to incur the responsibility of deciding as to the validity of the church rate in question. We therefore advise both parties to agree on a case to be placed in the hands of some eminent barrister, and we will adopt his decision as our own." On retiring for consultation our legal adviser counselled us to accept the proposal, "only," said he, "do not consent to have an ecclesiastical barrister: but [235] select any common-law barrister you please." He suggested to name of Sir S. Romilly, the Solicitor General, and after some little demur from the church party he was chosen as the referee: but on receiving the case he said he felt it right not to receive cases while he was in office: but mentioned the name of a barrister whom both parties agreed to recognize as referee. Mr. Richardson specified six objections to the validity of the rate. After maturely considering the case the referee decided that five of the objections were untenable, but that the one which contended that the vestry was really a prolongation of the vestry of the 22nd of June at which time the Kettering Small Tenements Act was not the law of the land, and that consequently the cottage tenants had not when the vestry commenced lost their right to vote, was a valid objection (the very one which I had originated) and that therefore the church rate was not legally made. I believe this was the last church rate attempted to be laid in Kettering.

On July 19th, 1848, I spoke at the opening of the [236] Baptist Schoolroom at Burton Latimer, and on the following evening at a Temperance meeting at Finedon. In August I attended the annual meeting of the Rechabite Executive Council at Manchester and to my surprize was elected Chief Ruler of the Order for the ensuing year.

The little chapel at Draughton, having as the result of a trial at Northampton Assizes been recovered from the hands of the clergyman, was rebuilt and re-opened for divine worship on September 14th. A further collection being desired I was requested to preach there on the next Lord's Day evening. The chapel and adjoining tent were crowded, a good collection obtained, and best of all I received a letter four or five years afterwards informing that a young woman whose remains are interred near Lichfield Cathedral, was led to Christ by the sermon I preached at Draughton, in the neighbourhood of which she was then visiting.

Although from the time that our chapel was cleared of debt, my people had regularly [237] given me thirty pounds per annum, yet greatly as I loved my flock, the increase of my family compelled me reluctantly to contemplate the duty of removal to another sphere of labour. Without either direct or indirect seeking of my own, the church at Oakham {Rutland] requested me to preach there on October 29th with a view to an invitation to the pastorate. I accordingly did so, and also on November 26th, soon after which I was invited to become its pastor, which invitation I, after serious thought and fervent prayer, felt it right to accept, though I said I should not be able to remove my family until June 1849.

On December 25th, 1848, I preached a Temperance sermon in the Independent Chapel, Brigstock, and on the following evening delivered a Temperance Address in Mr. Robinson's schoolroom.

[1849 to 1864. Jenkinson's Oakham years]

I had engaged to preach at Oakham on the first two Sundays in 1849. When behold, just at dinner-time on Thursday, January 4th, one of the Oakham friends (Mr. J. Barlow, Jun.) [238] came to my house, and said, "You are the very person I want. Our Library Tea Meeting is going to be held this afternoon, our friends are so anxious that you should be there that I have brought a conveyance for you." "Very well," I replied, "then I think I will go with you." Accordingly I did so: and a very pleasant meeting we had: addresses being delivered by the Rev. W. Bevan (Independent.), the Rev. T. Moxon (Wesleyan), the Rev. T. Thorpe (student at Bristol College) and myself. I stayed at Oakham until Monday the 15th. On the 31st gave my lecture on Water at Brigstock. On February 28th lectured at Newport Pagnell on "The Winds" [see Appendix 7]. On the afternoon of March 25th preached my farewell sermon at Kettering, Text Phil. 1.27, and on May 13th my farewell sermon at Cransley, Text Acts 20.32.

I was now, of course, a member of the Northamptonshire Baptist Association into which we had in vain sought admission six years before (see p. 210) and singularly enough had to preach one of the Association Sermons, which I did [239] in College Street Chapel, Northampton on May 30th, Text Luke 9.30,31. On the following evening addressed a Tea Meeting in the Baptist Chapel, Kislingbury. On June 28th addressed a Tea Meeting at Ridlington, (Rutland), and another at Uppingham on July 12th.

On August 5th three young men, the first fruits of my labours at Oakham, were baptized there and added to the church. On the 20th went to York to attend the annual meetings of the Rechabite Order, which were then held in that city. Left on Friday, and was unexpectedly mixed up with thousands of debased characters who had just left York racecourse. Slept at Leeds on Friday night, on which night about thirty persons died of cholera at Hunslet, a part of Leeds within a mile of my lodgings, yet by the good hand of God I was preserved in safety. Left Leeds about six o'clock on Saturday morning, and reached home for tea.

I have omitted to state that I and my family removed from Kettering to Oakham on June 22nd, until which day I occupied lodgings in Oakham [240] from the commencement of pastorate there on April 8th 1849.

On Sunday September 30th I preached two sermons at the opening of the Baptist chapel at Ridlington. On November 6th, addressed a tea meeting at Kettering and on the 29th took part in the Wesleyan Missionary Meeting at Oakham.

1850

On Wednesday, February 27th, my third daughter, my dear Mary Selina, was born.

On February 17th, I preached at Hallaton, and on April 21st, at Melton Mowbray [Leicestershire] for the first time. Attended the meetings of Northampton Baptist Association at Towcester, on May 21st & 22nd. Spoke at a General Baptist Missionary Meeting at Barrowden on May 30th. Preached three Baptist Sunday school sermons at Arnesby, {Leicestershire] (Robert Hall's birthplace: his father being pastor there for many years) on June 9th, preached at Shearsby in the evening. Preached to my old people at Kettering on June 19th. Gave an address at the opening of the new chapel at Slawston, near Hallaton on August 1st, the Rev. J. P. Mursell preached in the afternoon, and took part in [241] the evening meeting. Attended the opening of the new chapel at Broughton on August 8th, and preached therein on the afternoon and evening of the following for the purpose of supplementing the collections on its behalf. On September 18th, took part at the Independent Sunday School Anniversary, Oakham. Preached on behalf of the General Baptist Church, Uppingham, in the afternoon of September 30th, and took part in the public meeting in the evening. Went to Birmingham on the shortest day, preached five times in the large Baptist Chapel, Graham Street, in that town, on December 22nd, 25th & 29th, and gave an address at their prayer meeting on the 23rd. Resided during the nine days at the Rev. T. Morgan's, Senior, whose company and conversation I very much enjoyed. Returned home in safety by God's kind providence on December 30th. On the following day my friends at Oakham held a Tea Meeting in the Agricultural Hall on behalf of our library. To the astonishment of some, more than four hundred persons sat down at the tea tables. In the evening a public meeting was held in the same place. It was [242] addressed by the Rev. T. Blandford of Oakham, (Independent), Rev. J. Stott, Oakham (Wesleyan), Rev. W. Orton of Barrowden [Rutland], Rev. H. Whitlock, of Belton [Rutland], Rev. C. Williams, Hallaton (now of Southampton) and Mr.

Edward Jenkinson, Kettering, and myself. Thus pleasantly ended the first half of the present century.

1851

On Lord's day evening January 12th I preached a sermon in reference to the half century just closed. Text. Job 32.7

The Rev. C. Williams of Hallaton, having learnt from some brethren in his neighbourhood that a two monthly meeting of ministers of different denominations existed in Northamptonshire asked me if I saw any difficulty in the way of establishing a similar one for Rutland and its vicinity? After some correspondence on the subject it was agreed that we should meet at Barrowden on March 18th for the purpose of originating such a Society. We accordingly met on that day, appointed officers, adopted the rules, etc. which required every brother to write [243] and bring with him a critique on a given text of scripture, and one brother should write and read an essay on some theological subject. I was appointed to write the first essay. The text chosen for criticism being I Peter 3.18,19,20.

On April 23rd I officiated at the funeral of Mr. John Edmonds, for many years an eminent schoolmaster at Guilsborough, whose failing health had brought him to reside at Oakham with his brother. He was brother to the Rev. T. Edmonds, successor to the Rev. R. Hall as pastor of the Baptist Church at Cambridge. Their father was for I believe 30 years pastor of the Baptist Church at Guilsborough. On May 27th I attended a bazaar and tea meeting on behalf of the Independent Chapel at Ketton, near Stamford, and took part in the public meeting held in the evening. On June 17th our Ministers' Meeting was held at Hallaton. Present Brs. H. Toller (Harborough), G. Leman (Ashley), [Revs.] Orton, Amos, Hughes, Whitlock, Blandford, Williams and myself. The two first named [244] being visitors. I read my essay "On the Existence of evil evidential of the Divine Goodness". Every brother had prepared a critique on I Peter 3.18,19,20.

Our next meeting was held at my house on September 16th. Text for criticism, Gal. 3.20. On September 17th, I took part in the Independent Sunday School meeting at Oakham. On September 18th, spoke at the anniversary of Belton Baptist Chapel and on September 29th, at the anniversary of Barrowden Baptist Chapel.

A century having just elapsed since the death of Dr. Philip Doddridge[40], I, on October 27th, preached a sermon in reference to his character and works. Text Hebrews 11.4. (I find that I have omitted to say that the centenary of Dr. Watts' death[41] having occurred about three months before I left Kettering, I on December 3rd 1848, preached a sermon in reference to *his* character and works. Text II Samuel 23.1,2).

Our next Ministers' Meeting was held at Great Easton on December 9th. The brethren read [245] critiques on I Corinthians 15. 24,28. Am unable to give the titles or writer's names of any essays except my own (The Mr. appointed to prepare an essay for the meeting held in September, I read one "On the Knowledge which Disembodied Spirits have of External Things").

In July of this year Mr. Ashford, I, and Mrs. Jenkinson went to the Great Exhibition in the Crystal Palace, Hyde Park, and were highly delighted and greatly instructed by what we saw. After our return I preached three sermons suggested thereby. Texts Exodus 3.3, Kings 10. 4-10, and John 1.50.

1852

Our Ministers' Meeting was held at the Rev. T. Blandford's, Oakham, on March 30th. Text for criticism, Romans 8.19-23. On June 17th I had the pleasure of baptizing the Rev. Edward Hughes, pastor of the Independent Church at Great Easton. Our Ministers' Meeting on July 12th was held at Kings Cliffe [Northamptonshire]. Text for criticism, Isaiah 64.5.

[246] On September 19th I preached a sermon in reference to the death of the Duke of Wellington. Text II Samuel 3.38. The Rev. J. Twidale, pastor of the Independent Church, Melton Mowbray, having joined our Society, our Minister's Meeting was held at his house on September 28th. Text for criticism John 3.5. On October 19th, my daughter Louisa was born. Thus another precious soul was entrusted to my care. On November 25th I delivered an address at the Wesleyan Tea Meeting, Oakham. Our Ministers' Meeting on December 14th was held at Wymondham [Leicestershire]. Text for criticism, I Corinthians 15.29. I read an Essay "On compulsory Support of Religion not sanctioned either by the Old Testament or the New".

40 Philip Doddridge D.D., (1702-1751), was the distinguished minister of Castle Hill Independent chapel, Northampton. A theologian and hymn writer, he was an important early figure in the 18th century Evangelical Revival.
41 Isaac Watts (1674-1748) was pastor of the Independent Chapel, Mark Lane, London. He was such a prolific writer of hymns (some 650 of them) that he has been called "the founder of English hymnody".

1853

The first month of this year is a very painful one to my remembrance, as being that on which my dear father-in-law, the Rev. Joseph Ashford was removed from us by death. He had resigned his pastorate of the Baptist Church [247] at Harpole, near Northampton in October 1851, resided with us for a year subsequently, took at house in Oakham at Michaelmas 1852, and died therein on January 25th, 1853. He had attended all our Ministers' Meetings held after his coming into Rutland, and had often preached for me. I can truly say I loved him ardently. We never disagreed, even for a moment. I preached a funeral sermon for him on February 6th (Text II Corinthians 5.1) but was overpowered with grief when I rose to preach.

Our Ministers' Meeting on March 22nd was held at Barrowden. Text for criticism, John 19.11. On April 5th I delivered a lecture in the vestry of the Independent Chapel, Kettering, "On the Chemistry of Common Things". Our Ministers' Meeting on June 7th was held at my house. Text for criticism, Mark 6.17,18. On June 20th I took part in a Wesleyan Missionary Meeting at Empingham [Rutland]: and on July 6th spoke at the opening of the Independent Chapel at Freeby [Leics]. Attended and spoke at the Bible Society Meetings at Uppingham on August 2nd and at Oakham August 4th.

[248] Our Ministers' Meeting on September 13th was held at Mr. Blandford's. Text for criticism, Matthew 16.18. On September 22nd, I took part in a public tea meeting at Belton. On November 1st, spoke in Kettering parish church in reference to church rates: and in the evening of the same day delivered a lecture on Peace in Mr. Toller's vestry. Our Ministers' Meeting on December 6th was held at Wymondham. Text for criticism, I Peter 3.2.

1854

I preached for Mr. Twidale at Melton Mowbray on January 8th, and took part in the Oakham meeting of the Religious Tract Society on February 15th. On March 8th my youngest child, Albert Henry, was born: soon after which the health of the dear mother began seriously to fail. Our Ministers' Meeting was held at Melton on March 14th. Text for criticism Mark 9.9.4. On May 25th I spoke at the opening of the Reform Methodist Chapel at Ketton. The principal originator of that great Reform movement, the Rev. J. Everett, preached an [249] excellent sermon to us that evening: after which I walked home to Oakham.

On June 6th & 7th the meetings of the Northamptonshire

Association of the Baptist Church were held in our chapel. Admirable sermons were preached by the Revs. T. Marriott, J. Mursell and John Turland Brown. Mr. F. Barlow of Oakham being appointed printer of the Circular Letter written by the Rev. T. T. Gough, Mr. G. requested me to undertake its editorship. I believe it was done to his entire satisfaction, but the MS. was so rough and intertwined that both the printer and myself were in places sorely puzzled to make out its meaning. The brethren expressed themselves highly pleased with all the meetings, and with the abundant and warm-hearted hospitality which they found and enjoyed. Our Ministers' Meeting on July 4th was held at Kings Cliffe. Text for criticism Hebrews 6.1,2,3. On August 17th I laid the foundation stone of our new chapel at Langham [near Oakham], and delivered [250] an address on the occasion.

Our Ministers' Meeting was held at Barrowden on September 26th. Text for criticism Hebrews 6.4,5,6. I had prepared my critique, and also written the Essay required of me on the question, "Does Christianity Sanction War?"[42] But when the day of meeting arrived I was too ill to leave home. Mr. Blandford therefore took charge of and read both my papers. The Essay was greatly approved by the brethren, and requested to be printed, which was done: the London Peace Society having promised to defray the cost of the two thousand copies.

On November 9th I took part in the meeting of the Oakham auxiliary to the Religious Tract Society. Five days afterwards my dear mother-in-law, Mrs. Ashford, exchanged earth for heaven. I preached a funeral sermon for her on November 19th. Text Isaiah 3.5,10. On December 5th our Ministers' Meeting was held at Mr. Blandford's, Oakham. Text for criticism Exodus 34.7.

[251] Throughout the last nine months of this year the health of my dear wife had become gradually worse. Not only had she the medical advice of Mr. Neal, but also spent sometime at Stamford that she might be under the care of Dr. Pratt. Subsequently she went to Yarmouth for a fortnight or more, but being caught in a heavy shower while far out on the sands, she took fresh cold and returned to Oakham feebler than she left it. [*Added later*] She died on March 3rd 1856.

1855

On January 8th I took part in the Methodist Missionary Meeting at Oakham. On March 4th I preached a sermon in reference to the death

---

42 *Does Christianity Sanction War? An Essay by John Jenkinson of Oakham*, 1855, London and Oakham.

of the Emperor Nicholas of Russia. Text Isaiah 14, 16, 17. Our Ministers' Meeting on March 27th was held at my house. Text for criticism Genesis 9.6. On May 29th & 30th the meetings of the Northamptonshire Association of Baptist Churches were held at Princes Street Chapel, Northampton. According to rule I was the moderator: [252] and consequently had to give two or three addresses during the services. On June 12th our Ministers' Meeting was held at Belton. Text for criticism. Exodus 6.2,3.

Our old chapel at Langham had been occupied by my friends there through many passing years. Our last religious service therein was held in the afternoon of June 17th: on which occasion I preached from I John 2.18, "It is the last time". The sermon was much approved. Our new chapel there was opened for divine worship on June 21st & 22nd on which days the Hon. & Rev. Baptist W. Noel, M.A. preached three excellent sermons.[43] The Rev. J. T. Brown of Northampton and I preached there on the following Sunday. Collections were made after all the services. A bazaar was also held and a largely attended public tea provided. The pecuniary proceeds being highly gratifying. For two or three weeks previous the weather had been so unusually [253] wet that our friends were strongly afraid the opening would be a failure. But on June 20th a decided change took place, so that the whole of the days of opening were beautifully fine.

Our Ministers' Meeting on September 25th was held at Melton Mowbray. Text for criticism, I Corinthians 10.14. On October 14th I preached a sermon in reference to the martyrdom of Latimer and Ridley who were burnt at Oxford October 16th, 1555.[44] Text Revelation 12.11. On October 22nd I took part in a public meeting held in the Baptist Chapel, Barrowden, on behalf of their Chapel at Morcott, which had recently been newly fitted up. On November 4th, I preached a sermon in reference to the earthquake at Lisbon on November 1st, 1755, Text Matthew 27.54. On November 14th took part in a meeting at Oakham on behalf of the London City Mission. On November 28th, delivered a Temperance Lecture in the large Temperance Hall, Leicester. Our Ministers' Meeting was held at Barrowden on December 18th. Text for criticism, Luke 22.36,38.

[254] Although at times apparently better for a few days, my

---

43 The Hon. and Rev. Baptist Noel (1799-1873) was an evangelical clergyman of aristocratic lineage. From 1827 to 1848 he was minister of the Anglican St John's Chapel, Bedford Row, London, from which he resigned to become a Baptist minister. He eventually became President of the Baptist Union.

44 Latimer and Ridley were Henrician bishops, who were burnt at the stake as heretics after Mary I came to the throne. In the 19th century they were hailed Protestant heroes and in Oxford the Martyrs Memorial was erected to them in 1843.

dear Mrs. Jenkinson. has throughout the year whose close I am now recording been gradually declining, water largely accumulating in various parts of her body, and her strength becoming feebler and feebler. Her soul, however, resting safely on her God & Saviour.

I have omitted to state that my dear little boy, Albert Henry, wasted away in the Spring, and died in July. Having on account of his mother's illness he chiefly slept with me, I loved him very dearly. And yet ever since his death I have regarded that painful event as a wise and kind dispensation of divine providence, inasmuch as owing to the weakness of his loins there was great probability that his back would grow out.

1856

The Rev. T. Blandford having resigned the pastorate of the Independent Church at Oakham, and being consequently unable to continue his [255] secretaryship of our Ministerial Association, I was in the past autumn appointed to the latter office. His successor in the pastorate, the Rev. Robert Chamberlain, accompanied me to our meeting at Barrowden in December and returned with me from Luffenham station in a third class railway carriage, which being then uncovered ones, I believe he took a fatal cold, although the transit occupied but twenty minutes. At any rate he died early in January. On the 13th I preached a sermon in reference to his death. Text Acts 11.24.

On February 20th, I took part in the Methodist Missionary Meeting at Oakham. Our Sunday School having considerably increased, the roof was taken off our vestry early in March and a Girl's schoolroom erected thereover. We held a large tea meeting and in evening a public meeting on March 21st. The Crimean War being brought to an end, I preached a sermon on Peace on April 6th. Text James 18.

The more than two years heavy and [256] painful illness of my beloved wife terminated in her death on May 3rd. She was interred near to her dear father and mother and infant in the graveyard adjoining the Baptist Chapel, Oakham. Mr. Pinney, pastor of the Independent Church at Ketton preached her funeral sermon on Sunday May 11th. Our Ministers' Meeting was held at Melton Mowbray on June 3rd. I read an Essay on the Nature and Duration of Future Punishment. Text for criticism I Tim. 1.20 (The March meeting was not held, partly owing to Mrs. Jenkinson's illness).

The highly esteemed superintendent of our Sunday school, (Mr. John Barlow, Sen.) died on June 4th, aged 73. Only a few days previous he and I walked together in the procession of Sunday schools to the Tea in the Riding School in celebration of the Peace. No one having offered either him or me an atom of the abundance of the cake and tea that were there, I felt quite ill in the evening and was not at all surprized to hear of Mr. Barlow's illness and death. I preached [257] his funeral sermon on June 10th. Text Acts 13.36. (His brother Edward our very excellent deacon and my particular friend had died fifteen months previously. I preached *his* funeral sermon March 25th, 1855. Text Hebrews 13.7,8.)

On July 1st I gave an address at the Rev. Dr. Burn's Maine Law Lecture in the Agricultural Hall, and joined the United Kingdom Alliance on that day.[45] On July 6th I preached two sermons at Langham in reference to the Chapel Opening Anniversary. Texts Exodus 20.2. and II Chron. 6.18. On August 10th I preached in the morning & evening at Charles Street Baptist Chapel, Leicester, in the afternoon in Mr. Harris's chapel, Braunstone Gate. Took tea at Mr. R. Harris, Jun., my home being at Mr. Harris's, brother to Mr. J. D. Harris, M.P. On September 4th I took part in the meeting of the Oakham and Rutland branch of the Bible Society.

I have omitted to state that on July 4th, I took my three elder children to London. My friends said I should have them run over and [258] killed, but by God's preserving care we went and returned in safety: though crossing the thoroughfare was at time sufficiently dangerous. Amongst other places we visited, Lowther Arcade, the National Gallery, the Bible Society's House (the different storeys of which we were permitted to inspect), the Crystal Palace (where the fountains were beautifully playing), the British Museum, the Thames Tunnel, Woolwich dockyard, Greenwich Hospital, Madame Tussaud's, the Zoological Gardens, etc., etc.

On September 16th I walked from Oakham to Kettering before breakfast as I had done a year before. Having for nearly fifteen years been District Secretary to the Northamptonshire District of the Independent Order of the Rechabites, the delegates to the Yearly Meetings had from time to time deposited the surplus funds in my hands, on my promissory note being given for the amount. In consequence of an important and trust-destroying change in the secretariat of the Order at Manchester I moved five resolutions in reference to the dissolution of [259] this District, all of which were

45 The Maine Liquor Law, as its name suggests, was a New England initiative which aimed to allow local voters to close places where liquor was sold if a majority were in favour (the "Local Option"). It was the origin of Prohibition. In this country it was taken up by a new organisation, the United Kingdom Alliance for the Suppression of the Liquor Trade, founded in 1853 with the aim of taking Teetotalism into politics. The mid-Victorian battle between the Pint Pot and the Tea Pot commenced.

Figure 5. A membership certificate of the Independent Order of Rechabites, designed to be framed and hung on a wall. (*Editor's Collection*)

unanimously adopted, as was also the following, which was generously proposed by two of the oldest delegates:

"That in consideration of the valuable services rendered by Mr. Jenkinson as District Secretary during more than fourteen years, and the trouble he will have in calculating the equitable distribution of the funds, he shall be allowed to retain the sashes and other goods belonging to the District, and also all the interest accruing from the money invested in his hands from the 15th of March last."

In acknowledging this resolution I assured the meeting that I would make the requisite calculations, repay the whole of the money, and complete the business connected with the dissolution on or before the end of the ensuing month. This promise I fully redeemed, the sum distributed amounting to £102. 5s. 5d.

A terrific accident having occurred while Mr. Spurgeon[46] was preaching in the Surrey Gardens Building, I preached a sermon in [260] reference thereto on October 26th. Text Isaiah 2.10. Our Ministers' Meeting was held at Barrowden on December 2nd. Text for criticism, Romans 9.3 (We did not meet in September). On December 8th I took part at the Methodist Missionary Meeting, Oakham. Thus ended the year which, though to me one of heavy trial, did not fail bring a fulfilment of the promise, "As thy days, so shall thy strength be".

1857

Our Ministers' Meeting was held at Melton on March 10th. Text for criticism. Joshua 10.12,13,14. On April 9th, the beautiful graveyard adjoining our chapel at Langham was consecrated by receiving its first deposit: our dear friend [Mrs Sherwin] being interred there on that day. I expressed my satisfaction that the first grave there was that of one of whose salvation no one could reasonably doubt. Funeral Text, John 14. 1,2,3. On May 17th, I preached the Sunday school sermons at Gosberton, Lincolnshire, and stayed [261] to their Sunday school tea meeting, and public meeting on Monday. On June 1st I preached at Hallaton, and on the following morning walked to Clipston [Northants]. Attended all the meeting of the Association on Tuesday and Wednesday read and prayed at the large services, then walked every step of the way to Oakham, after supper on Wednesday. Our Ministers' Meeting was held at Kingscliffe on June 9th. Text for criticism, I Corinthians 3.15.

---

46 Charles H. Spurgeon (1834-1892) "the Prince of Preachers" was minister of New Park Street Chapel, London, (later called "the London Tabernacle") for thirty-eight years. A Particular Baptist, he was possessed of tremendous energy, and travelled extensively to speak and preach. He was the star Nonconformist preacher of his age.

On June 11th a special church meeting was held in reference to myself, which terminated to the indelible dishonour of those who rendered it needful (See page 300). In the midst of this and other trials, intelligence reached me of the failure of the Kettering Bank of which I was a creditor in the amount of more than £70.[47] Had the stoppage occurred earlier or later my loss would have been much larger. So blessed to have a God who foreknows all things, and appoints all things pertaining to us.

Some astrologers having predicted the approach of a Comet which would cross the [262] plane of the earth's orbit and perhaps come into collision with the earth itself, many minds being alarmed thereby I preached a sermon on June 28th in reference thereto. Text Jeremiah 10. 2. Our Ministers' Meeting was held at Wymondham on September 8th. Text for criticism Luke 11.8.

A Fast day was appointed by the Government on October 7th in reference to the mutiny in India.[48] I preached a sermon on the occasion. Text, Nehemiah 9.32-33. On October 13th I gave a Temperance Lecture in the Methodist Chapel, Newgate Street, Stamford. On November 3rd gave a lecture on "Observing" in the Corn Exchange, Kettering. On the 30th, took part in the Methodist Missionary Meeting, Oakham.

Our dear and valued friend Mrs. Allen, widow of a former deacon of the church, and aunt to Mr. Cave, one of our present deacons, died on December 9th aged 77. She was our largest pecuniary subscriber. Whenever I called on the day following our missionary sermon or meeting, she always said "I must give you my mite", [263] the said mite being a bank note for £5 (see page 301). The Rev. T. James, pastor of the Independent church, Oakham, died in the last week of this year. He was a good man. He rode with me in a gig to Kingscliff in June.

1858

I preached a sermon on January 3rd in reference to the death of Mr. James. Text, II Corinthians 4.7. On January 27th I gave a lecture on "Observing" in the Town Hall, Wellingborough. My journey hither by railway was, I believe, my first on the Kettering Line [of the new Midland Railway].

47 The collapse of the bank was the greatest economic shock to Kettering in the 19th century. John Cooper Gotch had died in 1852, and the business was in the hands of his sons when it was forced into bankruptcy. See Greenall, *History of Kettering*, pp. 111-112.
48 Fast days were national days of prayer and repentance decreed by the Crown and Parliament. They were triggered by events such as the shock of the Indian Mutiny, which were seen as demonstrations of God's wrath over the sinful state of the nation. Fast days began in 1832 over the outbreak of Cholera, for which there was another one in 1849. Others were occasioned by the Crimean War and the Cattle Plague of 1866.

On February 9th I received the sad intelligence of the death of my very dear brother, Edward. In all our movements in every part of life's journey we had been of one heart and one soul. He rode with me to Wellingborough on January 27th, and I parted with him at Kettering on the following morning in perfect health, so that in less than a fortnight to receive tidings of his death completely overwhelmed me. Happily neither the grave nor eternity had terrors for him. He was in all matters thoroughly conscientious. Our pecuniary accounts with each other amounted in the aggregate [264] to thousands of pounds extending through nearly forty years, yet we never had an instant dispute thereupon. On February 14th (the day after he completed his 55th year, or would have completed it had he lived 6 days longer). I preached a sermon in reference to his death, but was well nigh overpowered in doing so. Text, II Sam. 1.

On March 30th our Ministers' Meeting was held at my house. Text for criticism, I Tim. 3.2. On April 11th & 18th I preached at Trinity Chapel, London. Made my home at Mrs. E. J. Oliver's. On May 9th preached at Long Buckby. Our Ministers' Meeting was held at Barrowden on June 8th. Text for criticism, Matthew 2.15.

Meetings of Ratepayers were held at Oakham on June 10th & 16th in reference to a cemetery for the town. The clergy, the church-wardens and leading churchmen were anxious that six of the nine members of the Board should be Episcopalians. The Independent Church being without a pastor, the leading of the opposition devolved on me. Am glad to say we were thoroughly successful. We had previously selected nine [265] names (churchmen and dissenters) whom we deemed most eligible to become members of the Board, our principal point being to have no minister amongst them: our object being to exclude the clergy. We carried our entire list: and so satisfactorily that the leading churchwarden (himself one of the nine) said to me on the next morning, "You managed your business uncommonly well yesterday. I was opposed to your nomination, but I think we shall work well together." Eight months afterwards one of the principal medical men in the town (a churchman) said to me. "You nominated an excellent Burial Board. I have been on many committees in Oakham, but never found any that acted in such a businesslike manner as that does. Clergymen often think themselves very wise and know nothing. We have no clerical gentlemen on the Burial Board, and therefore transact our business so easily and satisfactorily."

On June 17th I for the first time went to Matlock Baths, taking four of my children [266] with me. We ascended High Tor and the Heights of Abraham, went to the top of the tower on the latter, passed through the whole length of the Rutland Cavern, and the Devonshire Cavern, visited the Petrifying Well, the manufactory of curiosities from the spar etc. etc. The weather was showery but we greatly enjoyed the excursion. Returned home in safety. Thank God for it.

On August 17th, I preached at Carlton, consecrated to me by the memory of my old and valued friend, the Rev. Charles Vorley. On September 7th I took part in the Bible Society Meeting at Oakham: and on the next evening at Langham. The Hon. and Rev. Leland Noel and his brother, Baptist Noel, being at both meetings, the first named being chairman at Langham. Our Ministers' Meeting was held at Melton on September 28th. Text for criticism, Job 19.23-27. Gave a Temperance Lecture at Melton on November 9th. [267] On December 9th I spoke at Religious Tract Society Meeting. Our Ministers' Meeting was held at Mr. Fairfax's (Independent minister Oakham) on December 21st. Text for criticism, I Tim. 3.15.

On the day I lectured in the Temperance Hall, Leicester (see page 253) I took tea with my friend Mr. T. Palmer, Chemist & Druggist: on August 10th 1856 (see page 257) with Mr. Harris, jun. I have omitted to state I received their funeral cards nearly at the same time, the first named having died on November 5th 1857, the second on November 14th of the same year, being shot by his own gun in getting over a fence and not found until after he was dead.

1859

On January 17th I preached at Whissendine [Rutland] at the re-opening of the Methodist Chapel. Our Ministers' Meeting was held at Wymondham on March 29th. Text for criticism, Hebrews 4.9. On June 2nd, I was appointed Chairman of a parish meeting at Oakham for filling up [268] the Burial Board (the Statute requiring one third of its members to go out annually). The three previous ex-members were unanimously re-elected.

On June 7th I spoke at Mr. J. Inward's lecture at Langham. Our Ministers' Meeting was held on June 21st at Kingscliffe. Text for criticism Job 22.30. On June 26th I preached at the Independent Chapel at Uppingham. On June 30th took part in the meeting of the Religious Tract Society at Oakham. The ministers of Oakham having agreed to preach alternately for a few weeks in the Riding School on Sunday afternoon, I preached there on July 10th & 31st.

The Rev. R. Wilson on being ordained pastor of the Independent Church at Uppingham I was requested to offer what is termed the

Ordination Prayer. Our Ministers' Meeting was held at Barrowden on September 13th. Text for criticism, Psalm 78.25. [269]   On October 9th I preached the Sunday school sermons at Husbands Bosworth, Leicestershire.

On October 11th took part in the Bible Society Meeting at Oakham. In the evening of the same day spoke at Mr. Inward's Lecture on Life Assurance. On October 23rd, I preached a sermon in reference to the death of the Rev. J. A. James of Birmingham. Text, John 5.35. On November 14th took part in the Methodist Missionary Meeting at Oakham; on the next day the same at Uppingham. Our Ministers' Meeting was held at my house on December 6th. Text for criticism, I Tim. 3.15.

A Literary Institute comprising some leading inhabitants of the town [being founded] I became a member of it. On December 8th, spoke "On the Character of Queen Elizabeth", on December 21st "On Capital Punishment".

1860

In the early part of this year, *viz.* January 18th, February 1st, 15th, 29th & April 2nd, I delivered addresses at the Oakham Literary Institute on the following subjects: "Gold", "American [270] Slavery", "The Comparative Advantages of Private and Public Education", "Were former days better than ours?" "The Approaching War with China", etc.

Our Ministers' Meeting was held at Uppingham on March 13th. Text for criticism, John 20.23. On Lord's day, April 29th. I preached at Hallaton and Slawston. On May 9th I spoke at a meeting in reference to the completed new Independent Chapel, Oakham. On May 15th I spoke at the British Equitable Life Assurance Meeting. On May 29th, spoke at the business meeting of Northamptonshire Baptist Association, held this year at Northampton. On June 7th, spoke at Wymondham Anniversary. On June 11th, took all my children to the Brass Band Contest at Peterborough. Attended morning service in the Cathedral.

Our Ministers' Meeting was held at Melton on the 12th. Text for criticism, Acts 7.53. Preached at Wymondham in the morning and evening of July 15th: at South Witham, Lincolnshire, in the afternoon.

[271] Took all my family to Scarborough on July 24th. Ascended the Castle Hill, rambled on the sands and rocks, bathed in the sea. Intended having a voyage to Whitby, but when we reached Scarborough pier the wind was so rough that the captain of the Whitby steamer

refused to start. But two steamers being about to start for Bridlington, we went on board one of them, were delighted much for about 15 minutes, when Alas! the pest of the ocean [seasickness] prostrated all of us save my dear Laura, and continued incessantly until we anchored at Bridlington. Though all the voyagers had paid their double fare at Scarborough many of them preferred to return by railway rather than by sea. Our nausea was as great in returning as in going. The wind truly was boisterous, and the waves terrific. But, by the Lord's preserving care, we all landed in safety. Were done over for that day, but ere long the following morning we were all right again. On Friday we all went to Falsgrave strawberry gardens, where we had a beautiful [272] treat of strawberries, sugar and cream. Returned safely to Oakham on Saturday, much instructed and pleased by our five days recreation. On August 9th I took part in the meeting of the Religious Tract Society.

The Rev. C. H. Spurgeon having engaged to preach at Oakham on September 27th on behalf of our Chapel at Langham, we held a special prayer meeting and several committee meetings in reference to his visit. The use of the Riding School being kindly granted us by the Earl of Gainsborough, we fitted it up with seats for the audience, and tables for the public tea we had provided. He came at the time appointed. Preached an admirable sermon in the afternoon, from Ephesians 3.19. In the audience were the Right Hon. the Countess of Gainsborough, the Hon. & Rev. Leland Noel, the Honourable Henry Noel, the Rev. Horace Noel, the Rev. C. Bagshaw, rector of Blatherwick, W.H.P. Owsley, Esq of Blaston Hall and Mrs. Owsley and some of their daughters. The evening congregation was very large, the sermon very inferior, [273] quite unworthy of the preacher, who however had a valid excuse in the toothache from which he was suffering. After paying the cost of advertising, printing, fitting up, labourers wages, etc., etc. the nett amount of the collections was £58, of which, as per agreement, Mr. Spurgeon had half for his College.[49] About 800 persons partook of tea (with which Mr. Spurgeon had nothing to do) from which the clear profits were £11. So that, by his visit we realized £40 towards the debt on our Langham Chapel: and a spiritual profit incomparably greater and more precious. I gave out all the hymns at both services.

As in the Lord's providence it devolved on me to inter the first corpse in Langham Chapel graveyard, so by his providence it was my lot to inter the first corpse buried in Oakham Cemetery. The Burial Board had appointed a young friend and hearer of mine, (H. Alfred Ellingworth) Clerk to the Board. He being somewhat, though not alarmingly, unwell in July, I repeatedly called to see him. On one

49 Spurgeon's College was the institution he founded in 1857 for the training of ministers.

occasion, he [274] shewed me the coloured plan of the Cemetery, the Rules, etc: on returning which I said, "Ah, and who will be first interred there?" He rejoined, "That is a solemn question: I sometimes think *I* shall" and surely enough, he was. He died while Mr. Spurgeon was preaching his afternoon sermon and was laid in the Cemetery on October 1st, a very large number of spectators being present. As we passed through the cemetery porch I observed the Notice suspended there, "*All applications respecting interments in this Cemetery to be made to Alfred Ellingworth.*" His age was 29.

Our Ministers' Meeting was held at Kingscliffe on October 2nd. Text for criticism, I Corinthians 11.10. On October 14th I preached a sermon in reference to the death of the Rev. Alexander Fletcher of London. Text, Ecclesiastes 12.9,10,11. On October 21st I preached the Sunday School sermon at Woodford, near Thrapston. On October 22nd took part in the public meeting held in the Independent Chapel, Kettering on behalf of the [295] London Missionary Society.

My very dear friend, the Rev. Jonathan Whittemore, formerly pastor of the Old Baptist Church, Rushden, [and] afterwards of Eynsford, Kent, died on October 31st. He was editor and proprietor of the comprehensive edition of Watts and Rippon's Hymns: also the originator, editor, & proprietor of the *Christian World* newspaper, the *Sunday School Times*, the *Baptist Messenger*, etc. Age 58. On December 12th I gave an address to our Literary Institute, "On England's Greatest Danger".

In July last, I took my dear son to the school for the sons of ministers at Shireland Hall, near Birmingham. Purchased a pianoforte for my daughters in September.

1861

Gave an address at Mr. de Fraine's Lecture at Oakham "On Funny People" on January 15th, and at our Literary Institute on February 7th "On the Recent Treaty with China". Our Ministers' Meeting was held at Mr. Fairfax's, Oakham, on March 26th, Text for criticism, II Corinthians 12.7.

[276] The foundation stone of the new Independent Chapel at Oakham was laid on April 11th. Though several ministers were present, I believe I was the only Baptist. In the course of my address I told the Oakham friends that having seen the plan of the projected Chapel I found they had omitted one thing, viz. to provide a baptistry. I said, "I believe you could in full consistency with your religious views both

provide and use one, and depend upon it long ere the chapel you are about to erect is demolished you will need one, or else lose your people."

On May 13th I gave an address after Mr. Henry Vincent's Lecture on Oliver Cromwell in the Agricultural Hall, Oakham.[50] Also in the same place at the close of the Rev. Arthur O'Neil's Lecture on Peace, on the 28th. On June 6th gave an address at the Rev. J. Devine's ordination at Wymondham. Our Ministers' Meeting was held at Barrowden on June 11th. Text for criticism, Matt 12.42-45. I read the Essay, "On Miracles".

Attended and addressed the Sunday [277] School Festival at Hallaton on June 24th. The next day, spoke at Mr. Collier's Lecture on Textile Fabrics in the British School, Kettering. On August 1st, spoke at the Religious Tract Society meeting, Oakham. On the 6th, at a Parliamentary Reform Meeting, Kettering.[51] On the 25th preached a sermon in reference to the Centenary of Dr. Carey's birthday,[52] Text, Mark 6.2. Our Ministers' Meeting was held at Uppingham on September 10th. Text for criticism, II Corinthians 2.10. I read and prayed at the opening of the New Independent Chapel on October 24th, and preached therein on November 3rd, at the last collection in connection with the opening. Text Exodus 20.24.

Gave a lecture "On Observing" in the Agricultural Hall, Oakham, on December 12th. On the 22nd preached a sermon in reference to the funeral of Prince Albert. Text, Jeremiah 9.21.

1862

Gave my lecture "On Observing" in the Corn Exchange. Melton Mowbray, on January 20th. Gave an address at the Rev. J. Twidale's Lecture, at Oakham. On March 24th. [278] Our Ministers' Meeting was held at my house on March 25th. Text for criticism, Matthew 12.36,37. Gave an address at Independent Tea Meeting on May 7th. Preached the Sunday school sermon at Melton on May 25th. Our Ministers' Meeting

50 Henry Vincent (1813-78), formerly a Chartist orator, now made a living as a popular lecturer. For 19th century Baptists, Oliver Cromwell was an heroic figure, the saviour of Parliamentary liberties.

51 Organized by the newly formed Kettering Manhood Suffrage Association, other speakers included the Rev. Thomas Toller, George Gill and Joseph Loasby, the secretary (*Northampton Herald* 10th August 1851).

52 William Carey (1761-1834), who began life as a shoemaker, was another Baptist hero in the 19th century. One of the founders of the Baptist Missionary Society, his field of labour was Bengal where he translated the Bible into the native language, in the process making Bengali a written language for the first time. He was made a Doctor of Divinity.

was held at Wymondham on May 27th. Text for criticism, Matt. 26.39.

On August 24th, I preached two sermons in reference to the Bicentenary of the expulsion of more than 2000 nonconformist ministers on September 24th, 1662. Texts, Hebrews 2.38 & John 16.2.[53] Our Ministers' Meeting was held at Kingscliffe on September 9th. Texts for criticism, Mark 3.29 & John 5.16. I preached in Northgate Baptist Chapel, Louth, Lincs. on October 9th. Gave my lecture "On Observing" at Great Wigston, near Leicester, on December 2nd. Spoke at Isaac Newton's (a negro) lecture on Slavery on the 4th.

Early this year the Rev. H. Richard, secretary to the Peace Society informed me that the Committee had resolved to employ a few ministers in different parts of the county to deliver occasional lectures on Peace: and that they had chosen me as [279] one of them. If I were willing to accept the offer they would give me a sovereign per lecture, and pay all my travelling expenses, together with the costs of printing, hire of rooms, etc. I hesitated to accept the appointment, but on consulting with my family, especially my dear Laura, I suggested that if I found the toil too hard for me I could at any time relinquish it. I therefore accepted the offer commencing my services at Brigstock on April 28th, Kettering ("How John Bull's children are kept poor") [on] April 29th, the public journals stated there were 600 persons present. Kibworth May 6th, Melton the 26th, Wymondham the 27th, Belton June 3rd, Bagthorpe, Notts the 23rd, Mansfield the 24th, Alfreton, Derbyshire the 25th, Sutton in Ashfield, the 26th, Wigston August 4th, Leicester New Hall, the 5th, Sheepshead the 6th, Mountsorrrel the 7th, Kingscliffe September 9th, Thrapston the 10th, Market Deeping the 22nd, Peterborough the 23rd, Stamford October 6th, Alford [Lincs] the 7th, Louth [Lincs], the 9th, Hallaton the 17th, Roade the 20th, Northampton the 21st, Kegworth November 3rd, Loughborough the 4th, Castle Donnington the 5th, Oadby, the 18th, South Witham [Lincs] the 25th, Oakham the 26th.

1863

[280] On January 18th, I preached a sermon in reference to the death of the Rev. G. C. Smith, the sailors' missionary, Text, Zech. 2.2. On the 29th gave an address at Mr. Russell's Lecture. On February 22nd preached at Roade near Northampton. On March 8th preached a sermon in reference to the Prince of Wales marriage on the 10th. Our Ministers' Meeting was held at Melton on March 31st. Text for criticism,

---

53 'Black Bartholomew's Day', which ushered in the ejection and persecution of the puritan ministers from their livings is a landmark in Nonconformist history.

Matthew 5.22. Spoke at our Tea Meeting at Braunston [Oakham] on Good Friday, April 3rd.

Preached at Stanwick on April 19th. Laid the foundation stone of the minister's house there on the 20th. Preached at Barrowden on behalf of the General Baptist Missionary Society on May 10th, and took part in the annual missionary meeting there on the next day. On May 31st, preached a sermon in reference to the release of Matamoras, recently imprisoned in Spain for distributing Bibles. Text, Isaiah 61.12, 13. I took part at the meeting of the Religious Tract Society at Oakham, on August 6th. Gave an address at Mr. Attenborough's [281] ordination at Uppingham, on September 8th. Our Ministers' Meeting was held at Barrowden, on the 23rd. Text for criticism, Revelation 20.14. Preached at Braunston, near Daventry [Northants] on October 18th, and at Walgrave on December 20th.

My engagement with the Peace Society terminated in April of this year. I lectured at Kettering on January 13th, Market Harborough on the 14th, Burgh (Lincs) on the 26th, Husbands Bosworth [Leics] on February 19th, Welford the 20th, Moulton the 23rd, Holbeach March 16th, Long Sutton the 17th, Spalding the 18th, Weldon on April 16th, Langham April 29th. The audiences varied in magnitude: but both in the last year and this the kindness and hospitality which I everywhere received from persons of all denominations was truly Christian. I believed considerable service to the cause of peace was rendered by my lectures: and the pecuniary recompense I received was of great service to me.

1864

On February 7th I preached a sermon in reference to the accidental burning of 2000 ladies in a Roman Catholic Church at Santiago. Text, Isaiah 47.14.

[282] What to me was our last Ministers' Meeting was held at my house on February 25th. Text for criticism II Kings 5.18,19. In the evening a public meeting was held in our Chapel of the purpose of allowing my ministerial brethren an opportunity of bidding me a public farewell, and also of presenting to me John Howe's Works[54] in seven volumes, edited by Henry Rogers, a *Life of Howe* by the editor being one of them. On a fly leaf of the first volume, Mr. Twidale of Melton, with the full consent of all the other brethren, wrote the following inscription "The Life and Works of John Howe Presented to the Rev. J. Jenkinson (on the occasion of his leaving Oakham) by his brother members (past

---

54 John Howe (1630-1705), puritan theologian, best known for his *Living Temple*.

& present) of the Rutlandshire Association of Ministers as a token of their gratitude for his valuable services as their secretary, and as a mark of their appreciation of his character both as a Christian and a Minister. Oakham February 25th, 1864."

For this acceptable present I expressed my unfeigned gratitude, and having solemnly and affectingly committed each into the special care of [283] The Great Shepherd this very pleasant meeting terminated, and we who had so often met parted probably to meet no more until we meet in eternity.

I preached farewell sermons both at Oakham and Langham on February 28th, and bade my people adieu on February 29th. Before midnight on March 1st, I left Oakham, walking all the way behind my loaded furniture to see that nothing fell off. Reached Kettering in safety early in the afternoon of the following day.

[Back in Kettering: Jenkinson's last years]

Gave a lecture to the Kettering Temperance Society "On scraps of Leather" on March 29th. Repeated this lecture at Rushden on May 16th. Kettering Temperance Hall being opened on September 10th & 11th I gave an address on each of those days. On September 19th, I presided at the Rev. J. Irby's anniversary meeting. On October 13th spoke at the Rev. Henry Solly's lecture "On Working Men's Clubs". Gave further addresses on this subject in the two following months. On November 15th delivered a lecture in the Temperance Hall "On the History of Gold Street", & on December 26th [284] another in the same place, entitled "Some account of Rose House".

When I left Oakham I thought my ministerial life was ended, or that at most I should only be engaged as an occasional supply. But it has not been so. May 8th, 1864, being the only Lord's day to the present time in which I was disengaged, and that quite accidentally by change of arrangement when it was too late to comply with any other of the four or five applications I had received. I preached at Rothwell, on March 6th, Steventon (Beds.) on the 13th & 20th, Kingscliffe on the 27th morning & evening, Nassington in the afternoon, Sharnbrook on April 3rd, Walgrave on the 10th, Princes Street Northampton on the 17th, Guilsborough on the 24th, Thrapston, May 15th, Desborough the 29th, Broughton July 3rd, Uppingham July 10th, Rushden on the 17th, Yardley Hastings August 21st, Walgrave on the 28th, Northampton September 4th, and at Stanwick on the other Sundays.

The friends at Stanwick repeatedly pressed me to become their pastor, and gave [285] me an unanimous invitation to the office, to which after long consideration and fervent prayers, I replied that if they desired me to live at Stanwick I must negative their request, if they would consent to my continuing to reside at Kettering, I was willing to accept it. Their acceding to my proposal led to my becoming their pastor at the end of this year. I had previously declined a similar request from the Church at Steventon.

Have since seen how kindly and wisely the Lord guided me, in leading me to resolve never again to remove from Kettering until I am summoned to a better world.

1865

Preached my first sermon as pastor at Stanwick on New Year's Day. Gave a Lecture there on January 2nd, "On the Protestant Reformation". Gave an address to the parents of Sunday Scholars in Mr. Mursell's vestry, Kettering, on the 5th. On the 19th gave a lecture in the Temperance Hall to Kettering's Young Men's Society "On Weight of Character". On the 23rd, spoke at Mr. Raper's Lecture [286] in Kettering Temperance Hall, "On the Alliance Permissive Bill".[55] On February 21st I gave a Temperance Lecture at Desborough. On March 21st, took part in the Northamptonshire Temperance Union meeting held at Kettering. On the 28th, spoke at Kettering Temperance Meeting.

The annual meeting of the Thrapston Sunday School Union was held at Burton Latimer on Good Friday, April 14th. In compliance with the request previously forwarded to me, I gave the Address. On the 17th, spoke at Mr. S. Smithard's Temperance Lecture in the Kettering Temperance Hall. On the 30th preached a sermon at Stanwick in reference to the assassination of President Lincoln. Text, Hosea 4.2.

Since the commencement of my ministry I had baptized nearly three hundred candidates. Gathered my first fruits at Stanwick on May 7th having on that day baptized Charles Green and G. Poole. On June 6th spoke at our Association at Rushden and at Kettering on the 13th, at the Manhood Suffrage meeting. On July 10th spoke at Rushden Sunday School meeting, and at a Temperance meeting in the open air, Gold Street, Kettering. Preached in Princes Street Chapel, Northampton [287] on August 20th, and at Aldwinkle on September 3rd at collection for repairs, on September 4th gave a History of Aldwinkle. On the 12th gave an address at the Temperance Luncheon in Kettering Temperance Hall, in the afternoon & evening spoke at Temperance meetings in the

55 J. H. Raper was Parliamentary agent of the United Kingdom Alliance.

Bowling Green, and subsequently in the Corn Exchange. On the 13th gave an address at the Band of Hope anniversary.

On October 2nd preached a Temperance Sermon in the Temperance Hall at Raunds. Text, Matthew 10.16. Addressed the Temperance Meeting in the evening. Spoke at Rothwell Temperance meeting on the 12th. On October 22nd preached a sermon at Stanwick on the death of Lord Palmerston, Text, I Corinthians 1.20.

On the 24th gave an address at Kettering Penny Readings, and on November 21st gave a lecture to the same, "On the Wit and Wisdom of Women". Mr. Usher of Bedford, having been an abstainer for 25 years kindly invited me to his soiree, at which I attended and spoke on December 4th. On the 13th spoke at public meeting in Mr. Mursell's Chapel in reference to Jamaica. On the 26th was Judge at the trial of Dr. Abstinence.[56]

[288] 1866

Gave a lecture at Stanwick on Dr. Watts on New Year's evening. On January 2nd gave an address at the Alliance meeting in Kettering Corn Exchange: on the 16th a short lecture in Kettering Temperance Hall, "On one night in Naples". On February 25th, I presided and spoke at W. Bonner's Reform Lecture in Kettering Temperance Hall.

On March 5th spoke at annual meeting of Northampton Temperance Society, and on the 14th on Mr. Bailey's lecture in Kettering Temperance Hall. Gave an address at Annual meeting of Kettering Temperance Society on Good Friday, March 30th. On April 2nd, spoke at Mr. Grubb's Temperance lecture, on the 3rd at Temperance Experience meeting. On the 10th presided and spoke at Mr. Mursell's Lecture in the Temperance Hall, "On the Human Menagerie".

Presided and spoke at the meeting of the Northamptonshire Temperance Union held at Kettering on May 1st. On June 4th officiated at the interment of Elizabeth Groom in the Baptist burial ground, Irthlingborough. Have omitted noting scores of interments elsewhere. On the 9th of July spoke at the Sunday School Tea Meeting at Rushden, and at our own at Mr. Welford's Lodge on the 10th.

[289] I preached at Thrapston on June 17th, and at Earls Barton on the 24th, and spoke at their Tea on the 25th. On July 4th spoke at Mr. Mursell's Bible Class picnic at Glendon, at Kettering Corn Exchange on

---

56 Presumably a Temperance propaganda play.

the 14th, on Lord Burghley's re-election.[57]

On the 19th accompanied our Band of Hope to Mr. Tucker's Park, Pavenham. On August 7th, spoke at the Reform Meeting in the Corn Exchange, Kettering. In compliance with the Rev. Thomas Toller's urgent request I gave the Address at the Union prayer meeting.

On the 9th preached at Burton. Collection for Chapel restoration; on the 10th spoke at Kettering Temperance Hall anniversary. On the 18th spoke at the Temperance Conference and public meeting at Finedon. On the 26th preached in the vestry of the Independent Chapel Kettering, and at 8 o'clock spoke at Lawrence Gane's lecture on Richard Cobden.

On October 9th gave a lecture on Glendon in Kettering Temperance Hall. On the 22nd spoke at a very large parliamentary Reform meeting in the new Town Hall, Northampton. [See Appendix 8.] On November 8th spoke as Chairman of the Northamptonshire Temperance meeting at Wellingborough in the Corn Exchange.

[290] On November 19th spoke at a Reform meeting in the Corn Exchange, Kettering, on the 20th at Penny Readings in Temperance hall. On December 3rd gave a Temperance Lecture at Ringstead. On the 13th spoke at a large Reform Meeting in Kettering Corn Exchange.

1867

Mr. James Wells having offered me two guineas for two lectures at Northampton on Parliamentary Reform, I delivered them in the Mechanics Institute, Northampton, on January 14th & 15th. Gave my lecture on "Observing" at Stanwick the 21st. Spoke as Chairman at the Northampton Temperance Union Meeting at Rushden on February 11th. Gave a lecture "on the Charities of Kettering" in our own Temperance Hall on February 12th. Presided and spoke at Mr. Mursell's lecture "On Epitaphs", on March 12th.

Gave an address at Kettering Temperance Tea Meeting on April 9th, also at Kettering Temperance Annual Meeting on the 24th. Gave the address at the union prayer meeting on May 6th. The last united meeting held in the old chapel.

57 One year before, in July 1865, the two Conservative candidates for North Northampton-shire, George Ward Hunt and Lord Burghley, were re-elected unopposed. The Liberals had failed to persuade the Hon. Fitzpatrick Vernon to stand for a third time. Kettering Liberals were disappointed.

On May 7th spoke at General Neal Dow's[58] visit [291] to Kettering. Moved, carried and presented an engrossed Address of Welcome to him. On the 14th spoke at the Northampton Temperance Union at Ringstead.

Gave a lecture on Parliamentary Reform at Moulton on June 18th. When returning on the following morning was taken so ill that I could scarcely reach home. But, by the Lord's goodness, recovered in a day or two.

Took all my family to the International Exhibition at Paris in July. Left Kettering at 11am July 9th, reached Newhaven in the evening, forthwith on shipboard, commenced our voyage at two in the morning. Had a beautiful run to Dieppe (the sunrise was enchanting), had an excellent breakfast at Dieppe (the gilded crucifix at the entrance of the harbour, the number of priests and sisters of mercy, and the women in a kind of night-cap left no doubt we were in France), went by railway to Rouen, visited Joan of Arc's memorial, then started by rail to Paris. Had previously engaged lodgings there, which proved to be very good ones. Took our provisions with us. Reached Paris about 6.00pm. Spent the next two days in the Exhibition with which we were highly delighted. On Saturday went over the [292] Salle Legislatif, many rooms of the Louvre, etc. On Sunday went to the Baptist Chapel Le Bons Enfant, returned to our lodgings through some of the parks & through the "Arc de Triomphe". In the evening, tens of thousands of persons were in the streets to witness a balloon ascent. In the morning & afternoon the shops were nearly all open, cart loads of stones passing along the streets, builders hard at work, etc., etc. On Monday we visited Notre Dame, the Pantheon, St Genevieve, the Invalides, the splendid tomb of Napoleon, etc. On Tuesday, the Pere la Chaise, etc. Highly pleased with our visit we left Paris on Wednesday afternoon; arriving at Rouen my family visited the Cathedral. Leaving that city we reached Dieppe about eleven p.m. went on board and commenced our return voyage at midnight. Had a fearfully rough and perilous night, were tossed about terrifically, and overpowered by sea-sickness, but through mercy reached Newhaven in safety, London in the afternoon; and Kettering about 6.00pm.

On August 1st, I spoke at the Sunday School Union in Mr. Mursell's chapel, on the 6th at the Temperance [293] Fete in Mr. Stockburn's paddock. On September 17th attended and spoke at the annual meeting of the Northamptonshire Temperance Union at

---

58 The American General Neal Dow was the author of the Maine Liquor Law and was visiting at the invitation of the United Kingdom Alliance.

Ringstead. Reached home after midnight, and Alas! found a letter in my letter box informing me of the serious illness of my dear Laura at Romsey. Have omitted to state that I accompanied her to London on her way to Romsey on October 6th, 1863. Felt the earthquake shock when in bed at Kettering on that morning about three o'clock. Spoke at Mr. Grubb's Temperance Lecture at Raunds on September 30th. Gave the address at the Union prayer meeting at Kettering on September 2nd. On October 30th and 31st presided and spoke at Mr. Bonner's Peace Lectures. Spoke at Northampton Temperance Union Meeting in Kettering Temperance Hall on November 12th.

1868

Spoke at Sunday Closing Meeting in Kettering Temperance Hall on February 4th: also at Mr. Jabez Inward's Lecture on Life Assurance on the 26th.

My beloved Laura left her situation at [294] Romsey in November: having for two or three months been attended without benefit by Mr. Taylor, one of the surgeons of that town. Subsequently she had several bottles of medicine from Dr. Congreve. Yet Alas! she gradually sank until just after midnight of March 2nd, (*i.e.* just as March 3rd commenced) she suddenly exchanged earth for heaven. She was on that day downstairs with us to dinner, tea and supper, and did not retire to rest until ten o'clock. She was interred in Kettering cemetery on March 7th. She was eminently pious, being baptized before she was fifteen.

On March 26th, I spoke at Mr. Mursell's Lecture in Kettering Corn Exchange. "On the Irish Church".[59] On April 28th spoke at Kettering Temperance Society Annual Meeting. Attended the Triennial Conference of the Liberation Society on May 5th & 6th. Prayed at prayer meeting held previous to business. Spoke at the [Temperance] Association of Long Buckby.

On June 21st preached in the Reform Methodist Chapel, Finedon in the morning and in the afternoon & evening in the Independent Chapel there for their Sunday school. On July 7th accompanied our Band of Hope to [295] Houghton near Huntingdon. On the 21st spoke at parish meeting in the Boy's National Schoolroom in reference to Kettering water supply and the cleansing of the West Brook: and on August 20th in opposition to the adoption of the Local Government Act.

59 For Dissenters and Liberals in general, the election commitment to disestablish the Church of Ireland was the big issue in 1868. This was done the next year. Conservatives feared, and extreme Dissenters hoped, that the Church of England would be next. But Gladstone and his cabinet had no such intention. England was not Ireland.

On September 3rd gave an address as chairman at Mr. Nightingale's (Junior Wesleyan Minister) presentation. Preached the Sunday school sermons at Hallaton on September 13th. On October 7th spoke at Mr. Nathaniel Smith's presentation at Woodford. On the 27th gave a lecture in Kettering Temperance Hall "On Phantom Fears".

Spoke in the afternoon & evening of November 19th at Finedon at the opening of their Temperance Hall. On November 24th went to Brettle Lane to poll for the Liberal candidates for South Staffordshire. On December 7th took a prominent part in opposing the adoption of the Local Government Act.

1869

I commenced this year under a deep sense of my responsibility and incompetency as [296] leading opponent of the adoption of the Local Government Act by Kettering.[60] Mr. John Stockburn and his supporters strenuously exerted themselves to secure its adoption. The poll of the parish was fixed for January 12th, and at its close the Chairman (the Rev. Henry Lindsay) [the rector of Kettering] checked the numbers.

For Mr. Stockburn's motion	315
Against it	422
Majority against	107

So favourably ended that struggle. Before leaving the school-room I suggested to some of my friends the propriety of presenting a testimonial to Mr. Eldred, one of the churchwardens who had rendered us very important service. The suggestion was at once adopted and acted upon. A silver gilt rose of the value of £10 being purchased, and presented to Mr. Eldred at a supper and meeting at the *Peacock Inn*. I being chairman.

[*From this point Jenkinson's handwriting becomes crabbed and harder to read.*]

1871

[*Jenkinson's health begins to fail*]
Went to Watchet [Somerset] in August. Spent a very pleasant fortnight with my daughter and her husband.[61] Ascended Brendon Hill

---

60 For evidence of Jenkinson's commitment, see his handbill by *A Hater of Thraldom and Wast* [sic] (Appendix 9).
61 Daughter Emily had married the Rev. George Waters Roughton, Baptist minister at Watchet.

on Friday the 19th, being driven up and also down in the railway truck. No steam was needed, the [297] truck ascending being drawn up by the descending one *et vice versa*. Returned on the 23rd, preached at Wellingborough on behalf of the Temperance Society on September 12th and spoke at Kingsthorpe on October 4th [and] Northampton Princes Street [Chapel] on the 5th, at both places on behalf of the County [Temperance] Mission. Regularly preached three times every Sabbath, besides administering the Lord's Supper the first Sunday in every month, when I was suddenly stricken down by paralysis while sitting in my study on Wednesday October 12th.

The stroke was not very severe, but such as to render me almost unable to speak or write distinctly, and this terminated all my public labours. In reference to which I habitually feel as Job did "It is the Lord. Let Him do as seemeth him good." Though on seeing closing the work in which I delighted I feel a wish that I could do the same. I can truly say that I have never had a moment of repining thought. Indeed, I have so many memories left that it would be base ingratitude if I had. I have not a large, but a comfortable income, I enjoy my food as much as ever, though of course I eat less, I usually sleep well, my sight and hearing are tolerably good. Though somewhat impaired, I can read, and enjoy my reading as much as ever, (Gracious God if it be thy will spare my precious sight and make me grateful for it). My children are pious, intelligent, respected and very kind to me, and amidst all my short-comings and imperfections, I [298] enjoy a good hope through grace that through Christ my Saviour my pilgrimage on earth is leading me to heaven. I have been an unworthy servant to him, but he has been a good master to me. For some weeks at the beginning of my illness I lost my hold of Christ. I prayed earnestly to the Father and the Holy Spirit, but seemed to feel no love of Jesus. In my distress I cried unto the Lord, "O Lord, make me feel more of the value of the Saviour's work and show me more of his glory." Very soon after this the cloud dispersed. The word "Emmanuel" came to me with such light and power as including all he is as God and all that he is as man, all He is in himself and all He is to us, that I have never once lost its savour.

This is only one of the many remarkable answers to prayer I have received: I will mention a few others.

[Reflections on his life and faith]
On May 1st 1825, having been specially helped in preaching from John 9.35. no sooner did I sit down than I prayed reverently that that sermon might be blessed to some sinner or sinners. At our church meeting in June, two of the candidates for baptism mentioned that sermon as having claimed them for Christ. In February 1826 my brother

Edward, being dangerously ill, I earnestly prayed that his life might be spared, and on [this] day the fever began to abate. In May 1838 I had lost my way near to [299] Brixworth and it being ten o'clock at night I thought there was no probability of my meeting anyone who could direct me. I therefore did what I have done since, stopped a minute to ask the Lord's guidance. In less than another minute I heard the creaking of boots coming near. It was a gentleman and two lackeys who gave me such directions as enabled me to find my house in safety. In the same month being about to descend into a coal mine in Staffordshire I committed to the Lord and He preserved me and brought me out in safety. Having been repeatedly disappointed and changed my mind in reference to marriage, I was very doubting and desperately alone within, under which the following words comforted me for years "Said I not unto thee if thou wouldest believe thou shouldest see the glory of God". And then I found it, for though Mrs. Jenkinson was not perfect, she was just the wife for *me*. After my marriage having been [on a] journey by railway I got out at Crick station (23 miles from Kettering). It was past three o'clock when I left the train and although it was February, I set off over the fields to Kettering. I did very well for about 16 miles but then got into a field from which I could find no way out. I therefore turned to my old remedy, prayer. On ceasing I heard the voices of two men who were crossing the adjoining field I therefore returned to the gate by which I had entered and there met them and was guided by them which way to go. About the same time [300] a friend of whom I had borrowed nearly an hundred pounds had resolved to emigrate. Having had recently to meet several similar demands which though I had met them honourably had considerably embarrassed me, I prayed that something might prevent his going and he did not go. Ten years after, there being again in pecuniary difficulty I again sought divine help, and a gentle-man of Northampton advanced me a loan which I two or three years afterwards honourably discharged. In 1857 a slanderous and wholly unfounded report was originated about me at Oakham. Some of the members of my church believed it, or pretended to believe it. The deacons were my friends, yet one of them advised me to resign my pastorate. To which I answered, "No, the report is totally untrue. If I resign they will say I was afraid to meet it. I therefore prefer to stand the conflict." A special church meeting was held for the investigation. I spent almost all the afternoon in prayer to God that He would bring me out safely. At the commencement of the meeting my opponents withdrew the charges they had been so cruelly and invidiously circulating, but then by availing themselves of the slander they had been circulating, they moved that my character having been brought into suspicion I was [illegible] to be their pastor. I implored them to state the times places or circumstances or at length to give the name of the persons or at least one person from whom [301] they had received the report: but they gave me no information whatever. But they lost their proposition, and I retained my pastorate.

In December 1857 our dear [Oakham] friend, Mrs. Allen, died. She was a good and benevolent old lady. I knew that I should lose her help. I therefore laid the matter before the Lord. In less than 48 hours after, a letter was written to me from Australia stating that the writer was the proprietor of a colonial newspaper who would be glad if I would furnish him with the name of some person who would undertake to write a letter for his newspaper once a month. If I would undertake the task he would be specially glad, if not mention that of someone else. I at once accepted the office and received the remuneration until my friend sold the newspaper which was more than seven years, indeed until after my removal to Kettering. Thus what I lost by Mrs. Allen was abundantly repaid. In 1863 the state of things in the church was that I felt that I would leave but had strong reasons for wishing to stay till the coming Spring. I therefore prayed that the Lord would guide the members of the Church to that conclusion, which He did. In 1865 I got onto a wrong path to Higham station and it being night I could not find my way, being a stranger to the journey there. After wondering about for some time. I again lifted my very voice to God for his guidance and again He heard me, for I almost instantly was [302] led into a path which conducted me into the right way. The number of these instances might be indefinitely increased but these are sufficient to enforce the inspired exhortation, "Seek the Lord and his strength: seek his face continually".

Another way in which God has manifested his goodness and care over me has been his fixing my lot and station in life without any choice or foresight of my own. When the death of my father had suddenly plunged us into the depth of poverty my mother eventually looked to her sister, Mrs. Waters, whose husband was a tailor in a good business in Kettering. I was with him 28 weeks, but his four children by his first wife acted with so rough hands that I would not stay longer. The next year, being under religious impression, they would not have done so. But the lot was cast for me. Having returned home to my mother I was at liberty to accept the invitation of my uncle Stafford (mentioned on page 19) with whom I had a happy home for nine years. This was the Lord's doing, not mine, as was also his bequeathing his property to me, which of course rendered my life's pathway much easier that it would otherwise have been. My becoming a minister was evidently his doing, as indeed also was my being a Christian. My settlement at Kettering, and afterwards at Oakham and Stanwick were wholly unprepared and unthought [303] of by myself. I neither wrote to either place, nor caused any other to write to it on my behalf. I did write and offer myself elsewhere, but the places at which I was placed the Lord alone directed me. This has been a great support under the trials I have met with. I did not bring myself there to be tried. My preaching the sermon on the Salvation of Infants in October 1826 was manifestly from God: as was also my visits to London in 1825 and 1833. My appointment to the office of treasurer to the first Kettering Co-operative Society, though involving large trouble and recognized by small emolument, but was incidentally of great advantage to me, was proposed by one of the worthiest men in Kettering, and certainly was never sought or desired by me. My purchasing my garden in 1825 rendered me independent of Mr. Gotch, my former landlord: also the visit of Mr. Dash, Senior (as recorded on page 112) and the kind offer he made, was evidently from God. The loan offered me of a legacy bequeathed to my aunt, Mary Jenkinson, in 1829, though of great use to me, was unsought by me. The same remark will apply to the Editorship of the "Kettering Magazine" subsequently. My beginning to preach, and my leaving off preaching, were the Lord's doing, not my own. I have said (on page 44) that "I was brought to Christ in the week that my grandfather died." I was laid ill of fever nine days before my son entered Regents Park College. [304] The above instances are not given as the only ones in which I have been directed and blessed from on high but as evincing the blessedness of having a God rather than being left to choose for ourselves.

The persons who exerted the greatest influence on the formation of my character were my father, my mother, my brother Edward, my grandfather, my schoolmaster (Mr. Buzzard), my uncle Stafford, Thomas Smith (page 70), Wm. Dyson (page 40), Rev. A. Fuller, Mr. Taylor, Mr. Edward Barton, and Mr. Cave, the two last named being of Oakham.

The Books from which I learnt most were Maclaurin's – *Statement [An Account] of Sir Isaac Newton's Astronomi [Philosphical] Discoveries*, Lord Brougham – *Introductory Essay to Paley Natural Theology*; Dick's – *Christian Philosopher*; Dirck's [Dirck Volckertszoon Coornhert] – *Philosophy of Religion*; Paley's *Horæ Paulinæ*; Ferguson's *Astronomy*; Paley *Natural Theology*; Edwards on the *Freedom of the Human Will*; Reid on the *Human Mind*; Dr. Payne's *Elements of Mental and Moral Science*; Dr. Vaughan's *Corruptions of Christianity*; Thomas Bridgewater *Treatises*; Rev. A. Fuller's Works; Dr. Chalmer's Works; Euler's *Letters to a German Princess*; Dr. Good's *Book of Nature*.

[305] I have seen or known the following persons: Her Majesty the Queen, Prince Albert, the Duke of Buccleuch, the late Marquis of Exeter, the present Marquis of Exeter, the late Marquis of Northampton,

Earl Russell, Earl Fitzwilliam, the late Earl Spencer, Earl of Gainsborough, Earl Pomfret, the late Earl, of Cardigan, Lord Liveden, Lord Milton, Lord Vernon, the Ladies Fitzpatrick. Archbishop Sumner, Bishop Marsh, Bishop Sumner, Archdeacon Trollope.

Clergymen: the Revs. C. Bewick, G. Fenwick, O. Fenwick, J. Dent, Edwd. Griffin Senr, Edwd. Griffin Junr., Dr. Johnson (Cowper's nephew), Legh Richmond, T. Grimshawe, editor of Cowper's Works, the Hon Littleton Powys, J. Wilson, T. Blundell, T. Brotherhood, T. Span?, Dr. Winshaw?, Edward. Bickersteth, Prof. Schofield, J. Hogg, John Hogg, J. L. Latham, Charles Levison, W. Whittemore, G. Bugg, Jos. Knight, B. L. Fletcher, Henry Watson, T. Vevers, Henry Corrie, T. H. Madge, H. Lindsay, (the last named seven were rectors of Kettering).

Methodist Preachers: Dr. Richard Watson, Dr. Jabez Bunting, Dr. Menlicott, Dr. Townely, Rev. T. Walker, Maximilian Wilson, T. T?, J. Brown, J. Constable, T. Pickering, T. Wilson, H. Fish.

Methodist Reform: James Everett, Billy Tawson, Jo Griffith.

Independent: Revs. T. N. Toller, Walker Scott, Edward. C. Lester, T. Toller, J. Fistin?, J. Green, George Gill, B. Hobson, T. Ne?, T. Brush?, B. Edwards, T.Harry?, J. Bennett, T.P. Bull, Joseph? Bennett.

[pp. 306-308 *omitted – long lists of names of Baptist ministers of Jenkinson's time in a hand difficult to decipher*]

[309] In the list of Baptist Ministers the name of Robert Hall deserves special prominence. Being a friend of Andrew Fuller and the uncle of his successor the Rev. J. Hall and in particular being the special friend of the Rev. T. N. Toller, he frequently preached at Kettering. I heard most of his great sermons those found in his Works. I heard the [beautiful] and [elaborate] charges which he gave to his nephew at his ordination November 8th 1815. Something of his character is given in his Works from the shorthand Notes of the Rev. J. Hillyard, but every intelligent reader who knew Mr. Hall could well see that the language is not Hall's but Hillyard's. The following is different from Mr. Hillyard's, but is more nearly Mr. Hall's:

"Further, be on your guard against aiming to present the gospel as a system, that every part of revealed truth is in perfect harmony with every other part the character of its Author forbids us to doubt; but the system of truth, though wholly present to His view, is but partially and imperfectly open to ourselves. As one of the builders of the inner temple you are required to do the work appointed you without desisting from that work for the purpose of reconciling any apparent discrepancies in the plan of the Great Architect. Bear in mind that the truth which He has revealed is eternal and divine, but that every system of theology is but human. Be not entangled in any [human] yoke of bondage. Pray the

Holy Spirit to lead you into all truth, and then in every instance give to you what you believe to be the meaning [310] of the text from which you preach, whether it accord with by any human system of theology or not. Neglect of this has led to the exaltations of doctrines and sometimes not those of the [illegible but possibly greatest] moment into undeserved prominence to the withholding or overshadowing of others of equal or even superior importance."

The following paragraph is wholly omitted by Mr. Hillyard:

"Beware of undue indulgence in the pleasures of the table. What we shall eat or what shall we drink are questions unworthy of great consideration by those who are sent to save souls from death. As the kind Master who you serve has given you the means of procuring many of the luxuries of life propriety will permit and gratitude to the giver will require that you should not wholly refuse to partake of that which He has placed within your reach but it deserves your serious thought whether some portion of the wealth which you purpose them to expend might not be more appropriately devoted to the extension of the Kingdom of Christ, or the mitigation of the woes of the indigent around you."

In June 1825 Mr. R. Hall preached an eloquent and elaborate sermon on Mr. Toller's meeting house from Acts 24.25 and as he reasoned it "on the Reasonableness of the Christian Religion, closing with the following splendid peroration:

[311] Every man that lives in indifference to the concerns of his undying soul and to the solemn and momentous future which awaits him is an outrage on the very instincts of his being, and an affront to everything which deserves the name of intelligence. For if it could be proved that Moses was an imposter and Jesus Christ the Prince of Sin the fundamental truths of religion would still retain both their validity and their importance, inasmuch as they are imprinted on every infant's conscience; are in accordance with all the deductions of enlightened reason, and are ineffaceably engraven by the finger of God on the pillars of the universe."

[*The final page is highly illegible but from it I have deciphered the following:*]

And now I have to record the close of "My Life" of active labour. I had preached at Stanwick three times on October 9th 1874 returned home in safety on Monday the 10th, whereto on the 12th I was suddenly striken down by paralysis slightly indeed in comparison with many but still sufficient to completely end my preaching and nearly so to end my walking more than a mile or two, and almost to end my writing. But the affliction is a [bearable] one I am mercifully free from pain, enjoying my food and can sleep soundly.

I am a poor sinner even at the best, and have no hope of salvation but through the merits of Christ Jesus my Lord, yet I have few regrets for the past and few fears in reference to the future. The Lord has [dealt] bountifully all my days. Though in early life I had two or three years of great poverty and privations my old age is spent in comparative plenty. I have had the pleasure of substantially helping my mother, my brothers, and occasionally my more [distant] relations, now though I preached more than twenty years without [remuneration] for my labour, I can truly say "I lack nothing". I have all my life enjoyed a merciful exemption from sickness. The only visits I have had from a doctor was the incident described on page 8 [inoculation in 1802] and when I had a chestiness of [illegible] in 1844 on which occasion I received a bottle of oil camphor for which I paid a shilling. A doctor has never felt my pulse in my life. Have I not cause to bless the Lord for his goodness and for the special mercies he has bestowed on me.

[Jenkinson then lists names of persons who had influenced him and books from which he had derived most profit, which repeat what he had already listed above on his page 304]

[Here Jenkinson's "My Life" *ends]*

APPENDIX 1

Documents relating to the secession from Little Meeting and its aftermath

[Unless otherwise indicated, the extracts below are from Fuller Church archives, Deacons Vestry, Blue File.]

1. *A letter to the Rev. J. K. Hall from a disaffected group of 35 people*. It is undated, but mentions a vote in which they found themselves in a minority. It is likely it was written in 1824.
Their criticisms of Hall are listed.
"We profess to be a Particular Baptist Church but some of the sentiments contained in these terms have rarely been exhibited in your discourses."
"We have been grieved to hear of Religious Experience being derided by the name of 'Cant'." "In avoiding Cant, as you call it, you substitute a chilling tameness calculated to check the best effusions of the heart."
They find Hall's preaching "deficient"
"not in point of talent perhaps but with respect to its nature". Speculative subjects have been raised, "and when the most important subjects introduced, they have sometimes been preceded by an apology, as though we attended the House of God, not to hear of the way of salvation, but to hear ingenious lectures upon what may or may not accompany it."
Hall's manner of preaching is also criticized. He did not, apparently, "speak from the heart."

2. *A letter of resignation from the Baptist church*, dated 10th July 1824.
"It is our humble opinion that one of the most Important Doctrines of God's Word is out of your ministry, or but partially Stated ... Namely the Doctrine of the Total Corruption of the Heart." This, "together with the Spirit and deportment of Mr. Hall will fully justify us in withdrawing and as these truths are found in our Brother Jenkinson's ministry we think it is better to Separate."
It was signed by Thomas, Hannah and Elizabeth Smith, Thomas, Mary and William Dyson, Nathaniel and Hannah Roughton, John Eyet, T. Curtis, and John Jenkinson, to which were later added the names of Philip and Ann Curtis, and Joseph and Elizabeth Law.

3. *Reasons for refusing to cooperate with John Jenkinson as a minister and for declining to reply to his letter to J. C. Gotch Esq.*, by J. K. Hall, 1828.

Hall refers to the "unprincipled attack on him in a printed letter addressed to J. C. Gotch, which he says is full of falsehood and misrepresentation." Jenkinson was admitted a member in 1822, and it was "by the springing up of this root of bitterness that many were defiled." Hall says that Jenkinson was a member only a year and a quarter, and for most of this time was a preacher. Hall refers to a public row at the meeting of the Baptist Association in 1828 when he was verbally attacked by Jenkinson.

4. *A Summary of the period 1822 to 1829 (the year Hall died)* (Fuller Church Book, 1818 to 1870, Fuller Archives).

It lists the names given above in Document 2, and notes that "in the end 24 or 25 members seceded." In 1823 the membership of Little Meeting totalled 170. "For a considerable time subsequent, the Church was disturbed, owing to the frequent attempts of the Seceding Party to induce others to follow them, but as there now remained none within the Church opposed to Mr. Hall, their efforts were unavailing."

5. *Letter of June 1841 from the Deacons of Ebenezer to the North-amptonshire Baptist Association.*

Informs the association that Ebenezer has 84 members and 80 children in the Sunday school. That "all bitterness between them and Gold Street Baptists" (*i.e.* Little Meeting) is now ended. Jenkinson says that recently the Gold Street Baptists have passed a resolution which has "completely healed the breach." *He could not have been more wrong.*

6. *An Arbitration on Behalf of the Baptist Association* dated 28th October 1842 by Richard Innley (or Inkley), Thomas J. Gough and E. Cave.

The arbitrators "agree in fully conceding to Mr. Jenkinson and his friends the right to withdraw from the Church under the pastoral care of Rev. Hall."
They "deem many things in the spirit and manner of that withdrawal deeply to be regretted and centured" – especially the following:
   "the great want of modesty evinced by Mr. Jenkinson and his friends in the centures at so early a period in their connection with the church and with the confused immaturity of their religious opinions they passed on the ministry of Mr. Hall.
   "the wantonness with which they trifled with the feelings and character of Mr. Hall.
   "The odium attempted to be cast upon the church from which they withdrew and upon the nature and tendency of the ministry of the pastor."

They offer the opinion "that no reconciliation can be expected to take place unless Mr. Jenkinson and his friends do fully acknowledge the impropriety of their conduct and publicly withdraw those statements which reflect injuriously upon the credit of the Church" and especially against [the late] Mr. Hall [who died in 1829].

They conclude that "the charges which were brought against the ministry of Mr. Hall are not at all sustained by the slight differences of opinion which obtain amongst ministers of these Calvinistic churches with which we are associated."

7. *A letter from John Jenkinson to the Rev. William Robinson* [Hall's successor], 3rd November 1842.
Jenkinson rejects the terms for reconciliation made by Gold Street after the Arbitration by the Baptist Association.

8. In *Ebenezer, or a Memorial of the Divine Goodness; addressed to the Church and Congregation assembling in Ebenezer Baptist Chapel, Kettering, on the completion of their efforts for the Liquidation of the Debt incurred in the erection of their place of worship.* Printed by T. Cook, Leicester, 1843.
Jenkinson celebrated the nineteen years of financial struggle to clear the debts on his chapel. He prefaced it with his version of the causes of the secession.

"The death of the venerated Fuller, in May, 1815, followed as it was by the ordination of a successor, whose character, sentiments, and preaching were very different from those of that justly celebrated man, was the occasion of grief which has never found a full expression, save at the mercy-seat of heaven. In Mr. Hall's ministrations there was much to admire, and something to approve, yet mingled with much that some of his hearers believed to be contrary to the word of God; while truths, which they considered to be of primary importance, were either wholly omitted or but sparingly advanced. The total depravity of human nature – the utterly lost and ruined condition of the sinner – the absolute necessity and certain efficacy of the gracious influences of the Holy Spirit – the value and glory of the Redeemer's righteousness – the unchangeableness of Jehovah's love – the suitableness and sweetness of the exceeding great and precious promises which he has given his people – were doctrines which were seldom touched upon." In the end "God in his providence permitted our nest to be stirred up, and thus led us practically to prefer His truth to the home which we had so fondly loved" (pp. 3-4).

And so, "Finding it impossible to continue with comfort our connexion with Mr. Hall, myself and fourteen others, on this day nineteen years ago, peaceably withdrew from his church, and formed ourselves into a distinct community – a step, which painful and even appalling as it appeared in prospect, I have never, for a single moment, doubted that to have been right; save that it ought to have been done four months earlier. Had I the past twenty years of my life to live over again, I should assuredly pursue, substantially, the same course in which I have been led. It is probable that for some time after our separation, neither ourselves, nor those whom we had left felt towards each other exactly as we ought. But I cheerfully record my conviction, that the majority of the members of Mr. Hall's church did not regard us with feelings unworthy of their Christian character. This, however, is more than can be said of all. Their pastor and some of his friends cherished toward us the most implacable resentment, and in almost every practicable way, endeavoured to prevent the success of our exertions. But these days of trial were mercifully shortened. Six brief years had not performed their revolutions ere most of our principal opponents were lying silent in their graves … (p. 5).

"From that time to the present the storm has gradually abated – I had hoped that the time had arrived in which the past might have been buried in oblivion. Fourteen years have rolled away since any, even the least, occasion of offence was given on our part. On the contrary, we have made concessions and acknowedgements to the utmost limit which regard to truth would warrant, and done all that we conscientiously could do to bring about a reconciliation. Yet after all we have failed. Nor is this a matter of unmixed regret. It is better that there should not be the semblance of union, than that the union should be hollow and unsound. The day of reconciliation will come; and ardently as I desire it, I am perfectly content to wait for it; – a sentiment to which I know that you will cordially respond" (pp. 5-6).

In fact, there was no reconciliation. In 1849, Jenkinson left Ebenezer for Oakham Baptist Church, where he stayed fifteen years. With their pastor gone, Ebenezer struggled. By 1864 it had been brought into use as a boot and shoe warehouse. Some people from Ebenezer returned to Gold Street. Not all were welcomed. In 1861 Nathaniel Roughton was refused permission to rejoin "considering his past conduct and present reputation." When they returned to Kettering, Jenkinson's daughter Mary Selina joined Fuller, as did other Jenkinsons, notably the family of his brother Edward. However, John Jenkinson seems not to have done so. He was and remained persona non grata.

APPENDIX 2

Selections from "The Kettering Magazine"

THE
KETTERING MAGAZINE
or
Literary Museum
a
Manuscript Periodical

No. 1 July 1829

Nempe igitur quae ad pacem
faciunt sectimur, et quae ad mutuam
aedificationem ... Romans 14.19

Title page of the first issue

Page 2

CONTENTS

Pages 3-8

PROSPECTUS

At the commencement of a new periodical it is usual to announce the principles on which it is intended to be conducted, the opinion of the Editor that such a publication is a desideratum in the province of Literature, and, moreover, that they have made such arrangements as will ensure the assistance of some of the most eminent writers of the day: but for ourselves (being as is well known somewhat eccentric in our movements) we must confess that we do not feel much disposed to pursue the customary course; and for this most satisfactory reason, that our path seems to run in nearly an opposite direction. The chief difficulty that other Editors experience, appears to be to find persons who think their lucubrations worth the perusal; we, on the contrary, could, we doubt not, find many persons who would be glad to avail themselves of the produce of our labours, but where shall we look for those who will aid us in their accomplishment? Other Editors seem to be overstocked with knowledge, that they gladly embrace every opportunity of exporting it to any point of the Compass, we, are so apprehensive of a Dearth of that important material, that for the express purpose of affording a secure and convenient Repository, in which we may preserve every ear of which we ourselves glean and every sheaf which our Correspondents may reap from their more prolific fields. Other editors apparently estimate the intrinsic worth of their Magazine, by the extent of the circulation, we, shall endeavour to bear in mind, that the value of a Store house is not proportional to the ground it occupies, but to the excellency of the articles it contains. Other editors may be supposed to pay some little regard to the pecuniary emolument attaching to their labour; all that we expect to receive (apart from mental improvement) is an increased demand on our limited resources, and an augmentation of our already numerous cares; with, it may be, a frequent sneer, at our Folly, at our Presumption, or our Ignorance. The productions of some other editors, though arranged in the printed uniform of Modern times, seem as if they had been found amongst the empty Crania of the leaden ages, but we, though as able as any of our Contemporaries to "call forth spirits from the vasty deep", and though clothing our publication in the manuscript habiliments of former days, are determined to admit only those amongst our correspondents, who have opened their eyes to the light of the nineteenth Century. On these our Correspondents we would impress the remembrance that our Magazine is desired to be a Museum of Truth; to Religious Truth we shall allot the chiefest place: whilst at her side, or in her train, Political Truth, Mathematical Truth, Philosophical Truth, or Truth of any other description will be found. Of our deficiencies and incompetency we are painfully conscious; but, with the assistance of our friends, we hope occasionally to furnish a repast, that will interest by its variety, please by its beauty, delight by its sweetness, and afford solid nutrition to ourselves and others.

Kettering July 1st, 1829

From the ***KETTERING MAGAZINE or THEOLOGICAL and LITERARY MUSEUM***, No. 2, August 1829, pp. 73-76.

ADDRESS OF THE KETTERING CO-OPERATIVE SOCIETY

It is a fact too evident to be denied, and too painful to be unregretted, that the poorer classes have in a great measure lost their spirit of independency. Our forefathers exulted in the thought that the labour of their hands was sufficient to procure the supply of their wants, without necessitating to apply for parochial assistance. But alas! this happy state of things exists no longer. The consequences are, a most alarming increase of Crime and an almost unsupportable augmentation of parochial assessments. Many persons have long deeply regretted these things, and at length a plan has been devised, which promises to effect the certain diminution of evils referred to, and which will, we hope, ultimately ensure their removal. More than forty societies are already established in different parts of the kingdom which are now in active and efficient operation; some of which have obtained land, and are affording employment to their members, And as what has been done in one place, may be done in another, we are desirous of adopting those measures which may, under the blessing of Providence prevent our becoming burdensome to others in the time of distress. We therefore on Thursday May 21st 1829 formed ourselves into an association called the Kettering Co-operative Society.

The object of our Society is, firstly by the donations of others, but chiefly by our own exertions, to raise a fund which may afford us relief in the season of necessity. As not only every penny which we give, but every shilling which we expend for the necessaries of life, will benefit our society; it is evidently founded on the principle of self support. Our application to others is merely to afford to our more wealthy neighbours an opportunity of shewing that they are desirous of seeing us raised from our present wretchedness and degradation. Whatever is given is most thankfully received; and we doubt not that many will perceive that assistance is most valuable which enables the poor to help themselves.
Kettering June 2nd 1829.

From the KETTERING MAGAZINE No. 240
Title page

THE
KETTERING MAGAZINE

A Manuscript Periodical

No. 240. March 1848

Volume the Twentieth, No. 240

Souls truly great dart forward on the wing
Of just ambition, to the great result,
The curtain's fall.
            Young

CONTENTS

Total Abstinence and Missions No.7; Eclipse in March; Astronomical Calendar; Guizot [French politician]; A Pytchley Ghost Story; There's nothing in vain; God save the King; Vulgarisations; reviews of Hinton's *Memoir of William Knibb* and Ashby's Farewell sermon; the Monthly Record.

Two extracts (both by J. Jenkinson)

A Farewell Sermon,
Preached at the Independent Chapel, Thetford, on Sunday December 12th,
1827, by the Rev. John Ashby, with a statement of facts connected with his
resignation of his pastorate.

This is, we believe, the maiden publication of the individual who may appropriately be termed the father of our periodical, the idea of it having been first suggested by him, its editor [Jenkinson}, however, had for nearly nineteen years to sustain the care and toil of its maternal parent.

Mr. Ashby has for more than eleven of those years been pastor of the Independent Church at Thetford, in Norfolk, during the greater part of which time he had enjoyed as much happiness in his pastorate as usually falls to the lot of a pastor of dissenting churches. Latterly, however, a state of things has arisen which led him to resign his charge, on which he preached the sermon now upon our table, which, though somewhat wanting in evangelical unction, contains many thoughts in as few words any sermon we have met with. The "statement of facts" appended to it, is sufficiently disgraceful to the parties to whom it refers. We are happy to hear that Mr. A. is now (we hope comfortably) settled as pastor of the Independent Church at Stony Stratford.

Monthly Record

[*On the 1848 Revolutions in Europe}* The democratic party in **Sicily and Naples** has completely triumphed. Although the troops under the orders of the king bombarded Palermo for three days, the people were invincible, the result of which was that at the eleventh hour the king dismissed his obnoxious ministers, appointed a liberal cabinet, and granted a constitution very similar to that of France. Whether on the restoration of permanent tranquillity he will abide by this concession is of course uncertain [*Jenkinson was right to be sceptical*].

Italy. The States of the Church [*i.e.* the Papal States] have recently been the seat of considerable political agitation.

France. During the past week France has been the theatre of most momentous events. Several Reform banquets having been lately held in various parts of the country it was at length resolved to hold a large one in Paris, on Tuesday February 22nd. Government though evidently not liking these demonstrations, took no decided steps against them until Monday, the 21st, on which day a proclamation suddenly appeared forbidding the intended banquet to take place. Its promoters therefore immediately postponed it, and urged the people to obey the law, pledging themselves to impeach the ministers on the following day, which was done accordingly. But the government by prohibiting the banquet had thrown a live coal on a mine of gunpowder. On Tuesday various riots took place in Paris, many of the National Guards going over to the people. On Wednesday the Guizot ministry resigned, but this being insufficient to pacify the popular mind Louis Philippe abdicated the throne in favour of his grandson the Comte de Paris, and nominated the Duc de Nemours as regent. The latter, being decidedly objected to the Duchesse of Orleans was nominated to the regency; but ultimately the people determined to have no king at all, and a republic was accordingly originated. Another of our predictions in our No. for August 1843 is thus fulfilled.

The King of **Denmark** has voluntarily granted a constitution to his subjects.

Great Britain. The second reading of the Bill for the removal of Jewish disabilities was carried in the House of Commons on the 11th of February, by a majority of 227 to 204.

Great discontent has been excited by Lord John Russell's proposal to augment the army and navy, and to increase the income tax from 7d. in the pound to 5 per cent for two years. We have heard that his Lordship has sett himself compelled to bow before the storm.

The Right Rev. Dr. Howley, Archbishop of Canterbury, died on the 11th of February, aged 83.

The Bishop of Chester, Dr. J. B. Sumner, has been nominated to the Archbishopric of Canterbury.

Kettering. On Thursday evening February 24th, a public meeting was held in the Independent Chapel to petition Parliament against the increase of the army and the calling out of the militia. It was addressed by Messrs. Wallis, Wright, Robinson, Jenkinson, and others.

APPENDIX 3

STANZAS
OCCASIONED
BY THE REMOVAL OF THE SOUNDING BOARD
FROM MR. TOLLER'S PULPIT

Not man alone but all material things
Are every moment hastening to their end;
The peasant's cottage, and the throne of kings,
And earth itself to dissolution tend.

Though some may claim a more extended span
As though exempt from Time's destructive power,
And seem to smile with pride at fleeting man,
Yet these must also pass and be no more.

Thus Britain's Senate-House, which long has stood
In all its glory, now in ruin lies;*
No more will regal splendour there be view'd
Or notes of thrilling eloquence arise.

And thou, old sounding board, art also gone,
For ever gone from thy accustomed place;
Thy period's closed, thy century's work is done,
And time will soon thy memory efface.

But not from every mind; for 'tis with thee
Some highly priz'd associations blend;
And where we look where thou wert wont to be
We seem to miss an old and valued friend.

Beneath thy shade what eloquence has blaz'd;
And thence what melting accents often fell;
While crowds have sat delighted and amazed,
As though constrain'd by some enchanter's spell.

Oft hast thou echoed back the welcome voice
Of some who long since reach'd their heavenly rest;

* The burning of the Palace of Westminster that year, which led to the building of the present Houses of Lords and Commons.

144

The fervent SAUNDERS[1] and the holy BOYCE,[2]
Who, cloth'd with grace, their fellow-men address'd.

Thou too, through forty-five revolving years.
Re-echoed TOLLER'S soul-subduing strains;
Whose prayers and sermons, mingled with his tears,
    Distill'd like dew upon the thirsty plains.

These are all gone; and gone are also those
Who have less frequently beneath thee stood;
For Time's resistless current onward flows,
    And bears away the evil and the good.

No more beneath thee pious DODDRIDGE stands,
Or RYLAND'S[3] thunders oe'r thy surface roll;
Nor FULLER urge again his Lord's demands;
    Nor HALL'S seraphic fire illume the soul.

Their voice is silent, but their works remain
In ransom'd souls around them near the throne,
And some yet left below; – for not in vain
They underneath thee made the Gospel known.

As by an arrow glancing from a tree
The Royal sportsman[4] suddenly was slain,
So has the shaft of Truth oft glanc'd from thee,
Pierc'd the hard heart, but heal'd its wounds again.

Yet strains or sweet or powerful, have not made
On thee the least impression, but have pass'd
O'er thy hard bosom, while thou hast decay'd,
    And still unprofited art gone at last.

Nor only thou; – for human hearts have been
Hard as thyself; nor more advantage gain'd!
Thou long around thee regularly seen,
Unchang'd, unsav'd, unblest they still remain'd!

And though, like thee, we may awhile have fill'd

[Jenkinson's footnotes]. 1 The Rev. Thomas Saunders, pastor of the church from November 1721 to July 1736.
2 The Rev. Benjamin Boyce, pastor from May 1740 to October 1770.
3 The Rev. J. Ryland, Sen. A former pastor of the Baptist Church, College Street, Northampton.
4 King William II.

A place conspicuous in the house of prayer;
We may from thence be for ever expell'd
To unextinguish'd flames, and black despair!

Not so the hearers who the truth embrac'd,
These will abide when earth and skies have fled;
Of perfect joy and purity possess'd,
And crowns of glory sparkling on their head.

One lesson more, old sounding-board, we learn
While we look for thee and behold thee not;
That soon we each of us shall find our turn
To pass from our accustom'd place and be forgot.

J. J.

Kettering, October 21st, 1834

TOLLER, PRINTER, KETTERING

APPENDIX 4

Kettering Chartism: a pamphlet

Our Rights: or, The Just Claims of the Working Classes, stated in a letter to the Rev. T. H. Madge, Curate of Kettering, by the Kettering Radical Association, 1839, Kettering and London, pp. 29.

Summary

1. "We (the Working Classes) claim to have a voice in the making of the laws under which we live." [*One man, one vote*]

2. "We claim that all votes for Members of Parliament shall be taken by [*secret*] Ballot."

3. "We claim the abolition of all property qualifications for the legislative office."

[Because] Members of Parliament "will be sure to legislate, at least in part, for the peculiar benefit of the class to which they belong,' He cites the fifty pound tenancy clause – the privilege of franking letters – the Corn Laws – the Game Laws – the New Poor Law. 'It follows that so long as legislators are required to be men of property, this exclusive legislation will always be against the working classes, never in their favour." [pp. 14-15]

4. "We claim that every Member of Parliament shall receive a salary out of the public treasury."

5. "We claim that Parliament shall be elected annually."

They note that "the most useful legislation" in any Parliament is usually passed in the last session, "We therefore claim that a parliament shall have no other session than its last."

6. "We claim that the country shall be divided into equal electoral districts."

"We have said that a majority of the House of Commons is at present returned by about 150,000 electors. This is owing to the inequality of the present electoral districts. That such inequality exists is well known; but it is not generally understood to what a degree this is the case. West Yorkshire, for instance, with about 28,000 electors, returns two members; Harwich with 156 electors also returns two members!" [pp. 16-17]

7. "We claim to be allowed to purchase food for ourselves and families wherever we can procure it cheapest." [*i.e.* via imports. The Free Trade argument]

8. "We claim that the working classes shall be exempted from all beyond their just proportion of the burdens of the state." [Behind this lay the dislike of such burdens as indirect taxes on tea, coffee, sugar and soap which bore harder on the poor than the well-to-do]

9. "We claim that the Church shall be wholly separated from the State." [on which Jenkinson writes a veritable essay].
10. "We claim the total Repeal of the new Poor Law, and the enactment of a statute that while it shall secure the rights of property, shall also recognize and protect the rights of those who have it not." [p.24]

Signatories to the *Letter* were "G. T. Green, brushmaker, chairman, and J. A. Leatherland, silkweaver, secretary"; however, it was written by Jenkinson, the Association's treasurer.

APPENDIX 5

THE CHILDREN'S FAREWELL
TO
MISS CHAPPELL
LATE MISTRESS OF THE GIRLS' BRITISH SCHOOL, KETTERING
On her leaving England for Jamaica

How many painful changes
  We meet with here below
But still the Lord arranges
  What'er we undergo;
Nor can we rightly question
  The wisdom of his plan;
Or offer one suggestion
  Of greater good to man.

Yet both the weak and stronger
  Are all tried in their turn;
And we, with others younger,
  Have sometimes cause to mourn;
Our faces oft with gladness
  Have in our schoolroom shone;
But now again with sadness
  We find our teacher gone.

A year has not pass'd by us,
  Though rapid in its path,
Since God saw fit to try us
  By dear MISS PRETTY's death!
And now another mistress,
  Who well supplied her place,
Has gone to guide our sisters
  Of Afric's coloured race.

She knew that God is gracious
  To black girls as to white
And that their souls are precious
  As ours are in his sight:
She therefore wish'd to tell them
  Of grace through Jesus given,
Whose blood alone can heal them,
  And make them fit for heaven.

O could our voices reach her
  Where she has gone to dwell,
We'd say, – Farewell kind teacher;
  And yet again, farewell:
May life be long vouchsafed you;
  And health may you retain:
Or when that boon has left you
  May peace with God remain.

On every new relation
  May he his blessing send;
And fit you for the station
  To which your wishes tend:
May you and yours together
  His sweetest smiles enjoy
And find your Heavenly Father
  To be at all times nigh.

May He your course unravel;
  And still your Guardian be
Wher'er by land you travel.
  Or sail across the sea:
And while upon our pillows
  At night we safely sleep,
May He control the billows
  And guide you o'er the deep.

Thus to your destination
  May He direct your way;
Then make your habitation
  A Bethel every day:
In all times of temptation,
  Or trial or distress,
May He be your salvation
  And shield you by his grace.

May all the seed you sow there
    Be water'd from above;
And saints by thousands grow there
    In faith and hope and love;
And may their supplications
    On your behalf prevail,
That heavenly consolations
    May ever with you dwell.

Farewell, farewell, MISS CHAPPELL;
    May God your mind prepare
Triumphantly to grapple
    With difficulties there:
Should wicked man endeavour
    To slander or oppose,
May his protection ever
    Defend you from your foes.

For all that you have taught us
    Our grateful thanks receive;
And when you wrong have thought us
    Our ignorance forgive,
And while you teach the negro
    To read Jehovah's word,
By grace divine may we grow
    To love and serve the Lord.

O when you bow before Him,
    For us pour forth your prayer;
And while you there implore Him,
    Perhaps He'll bless us here;
Then if we never greet you
    In this world any more,
We shall with rapture meet you
    On Canaan's better shore.

Kettering, October 29th, 1840   *J. JENKINSON*

[Price Three-Halfpence each, or a Shilling per Dozen]

TOLLER, PRINTER, KETTERING

APPENDIX 6

A printed handbill of 1848

Thirty-One reasons for Objecting to the Kettering Small Tenements' Rating Bill

1. – Because the promoters of the Bill have shown no good reason for obtaining it.

2. – Because it is a measure of flagrant spoliation.

3. – Because when anyone has invested his property under the sanctions of the law of the land, that law does not ought to be altered without far greater necessity than exists in the present case. If an alteration of the law is indispensable to the good of the community, justice requires that adequate compensation should be awarded to the injured party

4. – Because it is manifestly partial and unfair to alter the law of the land for the purpose of taxing one form of investment of capital while many other and more profitable kinds of investment are left untaxed.

5. – Because to enact a law of this kind for a particular locality is essentially unjust. If it be right to compel the owners of cottages in Kettering to pay poor-rates for their tenants, it is right that such compulsion should extend to every town and village in the kingdom.

6. – Because it is contrary to the fundamental principle of natural justice and Christian equity. "Whatsoever ye would that men should do unto you, do ye even so to them." Assuredly the promoters of this Bill would not like a number of their neighbours to combine to deprive *them* of a fifth part of their property.

7. – Because the risks and costs at present sustained by the owners of cottages are so many and so great as to render it highly tyrannical and unjust to lay upon them a heavy additional burden.

8. – Because many cottage owners are amongst the poorest of the present rate-payers, and it is both cruel and impolitic to augment the burdens of the weakest part of the community for the purpose of diminishing those of the strongest.

9. – Because the enactments of unjust laws is the most likely means of leading to the contempt and violation of good ones.

10. – Because the law, as it now exists, is amply strong enough to compel every one to pay poor-rates who can and ought to pay them. The only reason why this has not been done is the remissness of the overseers [of the poor].

11. – Because far more honest means are easily available for alleviating the pressure of the poor-rates upon those who are justly entitled to complain of their present amount.

12. – Because unjust as it is to require cottage owners to pay poor-rates for their tenants the owners in Kettering have, for the sake of preventing animosity in the town in which they live, voluntarily offered to pay a liberal composition rate. There is no reason to suppose that one of them would dissent from this offer, but if any should do so, the parish could enforce it upon him with far less difficulty than it will find in carrying the proposed law into effect.

13. – Because the passing of this Bill will to a great extent, if not entirely, terminate the erection of comfortable and healthy cottages for the poor of Kettering, although without such cottages all other arrangements for the sanitary improvement of the town will be comparatively worthless.

14. – Because a considerable part of the burden will eventually fall upon the tenants of cottages, most are so poor as to find great difficulty in paying their present amount of rent. Many of the promoters of this Bill do not wish thereby to injure the cottage owner, but adopt it as an underhand means of compelling the working classes to pay poor-rates.

15. – Because to bring their amount of rent within the reach of their limited means the poor will be driven to reside by two or three families in one cottage, to the manifest injury of their health, and the consequent origination of diseases to which others besides the poor may fall victims.

16. – Because more than a third of the non-ratepaying cottages are occupied by persons receiving parochial relief, who cannot pay poor-rates, either directly or indirectly, without an increased allowance.

17. – Because nearly another third are occupied by tenants who, though they have striven earnestly and long to avoid becoming paupers, will, if they are in any way compelled to pay poor-rates, be necessitated to apply for parochial aid.

18. – Because it will render it impossible for cottage owners to extend that forbearance to their tenants which they have been accustomed to show, and without which many will be deprived of their homes and compelled to shelter in the workhouse, to the manifest increase of the poor-rates.

19. – Because our town is so poor as to render it exceedingly unwise to expend any portion of its funds in attempting to procure a needless Act of Parliament.

20. – Because it is probable that this Bill, if applied for, will not pass the Legislature, and thus all the money expended upon it will be worse than wasted.

21. – Because while this attempt is certain to take money out of the town it will not, in any case bring a shilling into it.

22. – Because even if the Act is obtained, it is morally certain to disappoint the expectations of its promoters.

23. – Because in other places for which a similar act has bee procured it is found to be productive of great evil.

24. – Because whilst a tradesman or tenant farmer who thinks himself

unduly rated can remove to a more fairly-dealing parish, a cottage owner's property being fixed, he has no such means of relieving himself from the imposition.

25. – Because it is very likely to involve the cost, trouble and vexation of a new rating of the parish.

26. – Because it will, in various other ways, inflict injury upon our town,

27. – Because it will occasion one of the worst evils of civil commotion, viz., diminishing confidence in the security of property.

28. – Because there is reason to believe that at least four-fifths of the inhabitants of the town are opposed to it.

29. – Because the promoters of the Bill have refused the rate-payers an opportunity of procuring copies of it, previous to signifying their approval of it in the parish vestry.

30. – Because scarcely half a dozen of the rate-payers have seen it, and merely a small proportion have even heard it read, and they only once.

31. – Because when a poll of the parish was respectfully demanded for the purpose of ascertaining how far the Bill was approved by the rate-payers at large, the chairman of the vestry, under the guidance of some of the principal promoters of the Bill, refused to grant that unquestionably legal and reasonable demand.

"I SPEAK AS UNTO WISE MEN; JUDGE YE WHAT I SAY"

A RATE-PAYER

Ayer, Printer, Leicester

This handbill is in the collection in the Local Studies Room, Northamptonshire Libraries and Information Service, Abington Street, Northampton. Above **A RATE-PAYER** is inserted "J. Jenkinson", in his hand.

APPENDIX 7

A poster advertising one of John Jenkinson's stock lectures.

NEWPORT PAGNELL
Literary and Scientific Institution
A LECTURE
Being the seventh of the season will be delivered to the members of this Institution by

REV. JOHN JENKINSON
ON THE WINDS
At the Public Room, Newport Pagnell
ON WEDNESDAY EVENING, February the 28th, 1849

SYLLABUS

Introductory Remarks.
Wind, air in motion.
General Cause of Wind.
Sea Breezes.
Land Breezes.
Trade Winds and Monsoons.
The Kamsin, Samiel, Simoon and Sirocco.
Different velocities of the Wind.
Storms, Hurricanes, Tornadoes, Whirlwinds, &c.
Equinoctal Gales.
The uncertainty of the wind more apparent than real.
Why a strong Wind depresses the Barometer.
Illustrations which the Wind presents of Divine Wisdom and goodness.
Utility of the wind as a meteorological agent.
Conclusion.

The lecture to commence at HALF-PAST SEVEN o'clock precisely

TICKETS, One Shilling each to non-Subscribers, may be had at **TITE'S** Printing Office, St John Street and at the door of the Public Room.

PRINTED AT TITE'S OFFICE, ST. JOHN STREET, NEWPORT

APPENDIX 8

The *Northampton Mercury* of 27th October 1866 reports Jenkinson's speech at a "Great Reform Demonstration in Northampton."

The REV. JOHN JENKINSON of Kettering, commenced by addressing the assembly as brother Reformers, and the Conservatives in the gallery as brother anti-Reformers (Laughter). He was glad to be with them at their Reform school, and was glad to see that they had got some new scholars (Laughter). Sixty-one years ago Nelson hoisted his memorable signal at the masthead of the Victory – "England expects that every man this day will do his duty." That was the Reformers' motto that day, and they had hoisted it on board the Victory. They meant to go on to that Victory. They meant to go on until every opponent acknowledged that they were right (Hear, hear). It was important in every step they took to be to be on the right side. Be on the right side, and it would be fair and free for everything that was done. Truth must never fear (Hear, hear). It was no new thing for him to take part in Reform meetings. He was neither a young man nor a young Reformer. He had publicly on the platform and in the Press and the pulpit for more than thirty years advocated the principles of Reform. Their motto at Kettering was "Justice to all" and that was injustice that night. He was glad that there were persons amongst them that night who were members of the Radical Association thirty years ago, and who had maintained intact their principles ever since. There were few things more gratifying than to find, that the principles one cherished amid the storms, when all classes well nigh, except for a few working man, were opposed to them, making headway and becoming popular, or forgotten because they had been realized (Hear hear). He had not held those principles for more than thirty years without having some substantial reason for it. He need not advert to the principle of right. His great point was that every man ought to have a vote for a Member of Parliament because it was his right. That was the foundation that night. Two eminent gentlemen stated that afternoon that it was a legal right that every man who paid taxes should have a voice in the election of their representatives; and he was sure that it was a moral and scriptural right. Without entering into the question of right, he would mark two objections that were brought against the extension of the suffrage.

It had been said in the House of Commons that the people did not want Reform. It was stated there was proof that the people did not want Reform. And, as an instance it was said that a great many mechanics who earned their thirty shillings a week, could well afford to live in £10 houses, rented only £7 or £8 houses. There were others in the country who might have a vote, but were not sufficiently interested to spend £30 or £40 in order to purchase the right and therefore were not entitled to a vote. He, however, knew that the reason they did not vote was because no man liked to buy what he had a right to (Cheers). Supposing they were charged 6d. apiece once a year to go down the streets once a year. It would not be that they grudged the money that they complained of, but that they thought they had a right to walk the streets independently of any payment (Hear, hear). The working man did not like to buy that which he had a right to. He was like a man buying the use of his own limbs, his thoughts or his eyes (Cheers). He had a right to have a voice in the election of his representatives in Parliament. Six children should grow up side by side, be taught at the same school, yet five of them in after life should not be allowed to take part in the choice of a representative in Parliament. Was it not preposterous? That state of things must come to an end.

Then there was another objection. If the people get votes they will make a bad use of them, it was said ("Oh!" "Oh!"). In some cases some well-meaning persons would say to individuals of their acquaintance, "Why, Tom, what use would you make of it?" It was the man's right to decide what use he would make of his vote (Hear, hear). He thought some who held large estates would find it difficult to prove their right if it depended on the way they used their income (Laughter and cheers). He knew that some working men were not as good as they ought to be, but he knew also that it was the same with the upper classes (Cheers). All the inebriety and vice in the world were not found on shoemakers' seats, but they were also found in higher quarters. And he knew that a policeman would take a poor drunken man to the lock-up when he would not take a rich drunken man thither (Hear, hear and cheers). The fact was that those who objected to the measure judged people by their own standards (A laugh). They imagined what they should do under the same circumstances, and imagined that the poor people were as bad as they (Laughter and cheers). He was not going to flatter the poor, but he would say that they had a lot of common honesty. He had to do with rich people with jewelled rings on their finger, but he had lost a good deal more by the jewelled rings – (laughter) – or rather in that quarter, than in the other. But it was said that the matter was not to be settled exactly on the ground of right, and that in all affairs they must take expediency into consideration as well as the right. If they gave up right for the sake of expediency then he opposed it. They could not be truly wise if they sacrificed right to expediency (Hear, hear). Every man has a right to the suffrage, and every man ought to have it on the grounds of expediency and sound policy (Hear, hear).

Then if they wanted facts they could have them. It had so occurred that in this country Members of Parliament were returned in constituencies varying from very large numbers to very small ones indeed. It was said of the honourable member for Calne, that the Marquis of Lansdowne was his real constituent, and he was now dead. And it was generally from such small places that ignorant members were returned. Let them compare Birmingham, Leeds, Bradford, London or Northampton with Totnes, Andover, and Thetford. Did they find the best men returned by those towns? Those small boroughs were in the hands of the aristocracy to a great extent (Hear, hear). When a certain nobleman wanted something from the Government he could not get, he said "Remember we are seven." And seven was a considerable number in the opposition scale. The House of Commons ought not to be the House of Lords (Hear, hear). The House of Lords was theirs. But the House of Commons was the people's (Hear, hear). It was true there was something egregiously absurd in the amount of land held by these people. Mr. Bright stated that 150 men owned half the land of England, and not more than 10 or 12 men owned half the land of Scotland. He would not rob them of their estates but they could not help saying that it was a shame to take away the poor man's right to vote how he pleased when he thought to rectify the wrongs under which the country suffered. They were only a thing it was said, but they were men when they obeyed or disobeyed the law, and when taxes were placed on them for their sugar and tea (Hear, hear). They had no more of a vote than their tea-kettle had (Laughter).

He asked whether such should be the case, and whether it were for the honour of the country ("No, no"). They might depend upon it that such a state of things could not exist much longer (Hear, hear). They owed their Conservative friends a great deal in that matter. If it had not been their very unwise opposition in the last Session, the question of Manhood Suffrage would have been staved off for another 20 years. But now it would not be so. (Hear, hear.) He had advised his friends of Kettering to ask for all they wanted, and to keep all they could get (Laughter and cheers). But his advice was different now "Ask all you want, but don't take the paltry pittance they offered then." Let them maintain the battle. They might depend upon it, for they had everything good, scripturally, morally and politically on their side and their Conservative friends knew it. When and where did they call a large meeting such as that in Northampton. When and where did they call a large assembly in order that the people might say that Reform was not wanted. Nowhere! Knowledge was increasing, although education was not what it should be, and what it would be. Still, the people were much better educated than they were forty years ago. Notwithstanding the opposition of the Conservative Party, they had got cheap knowledge, and the people could not now be cheated as they were formerly (Hear,

hear). One thing the Conservatives had forgotten, and that was, that though an intelligent people was more easy to govern well then an ignorant people, yet it was far harder to govern unjustly (Hear, hear). The more knowledge the people got the harder was it to keep them down. But their friends would not wish to keep them down by physical force, and if they were to keep them down by moral force they must find better arguments (Hear, hear). He had just looked at the *Northampton Herald* the other day, and found that a man could not take a certain medicine, because it performed a Radical cure. He did not despair of seeing the Conservative gentlemen taking the lead in Reform meetings yet (Laughter). And whether they liked it or not it would be done. If they did part of the work they should have part of the honour, but if they refused the work they must be content to go without the honour. Some persons came in when the battle had been won, and said "What a famous victory we have won" (Laughter). He did not like Reformers of that character much, though it was better late than never. They tried to stop the uprising tide, the uprising sun, but they would not manage it. They were trying to stop Reform, but time was against them, and the more they opposed it, the faster and the surer would it go on – (Hear, hear) – until the people were educated by being electors. When a man had no vote or voice in public matters he felt no interest in them; but once give him a vote and that interest was rekindled in his spirit. He hoped it would be not a long time such an assembly could be again gathered in as large, or larger numbers than on that day, to shout "Reform has been sought for and Reform has been gained" (Loud cheers).

APPENDIX 9

[A handbill]

LOCAL GOVERNMENT ACT
TO THE
RATE-PAYERS
OF KETTERING

Friends and Neighbours,

The "Local Government Act" which strenuous efforts are now being made to induce you to adopt will render you liable to the payment of Rates much larger than you are at present paying.

It will, moreover, almost certainly lead to reckless expenditure and waste of the money you will be required to pay.

It will also enable the Board to borrow money more than seventeen thousand pounds without your sanction or consent, and compel you to defray both the principal and the interest of that sum.

Some of you who are occupiers of Land imagine that the Act will reduce your payments. Its actual operation will awake you from your pleasing dream. It will avail you nothing to exclaim thereafter, "Had we known that our rates would be so much increased we would not have voted for the adoption of the Act."

Although the poorest man in Kettering is eligible for election to the Imperial Parliament, and thus to vote away scores of millions of pounds from the National Exchequer, no none can be elected a Member of a Local Government Board unless he is worth £500 or rated at £15 per annum. Thus the very persons on which the rates press most heavily are excluded from the Board which expends the money.

It is, in brief, an Act for the aggrandizement of the wealthy at the cost of their poorer neighbours.

In addition to the increased rates to which it will render you liable, the Act will place you under an odious and vexatious domination, which the recent history of our town shews likely to be exercised with partiality and want of discretion.

The improvements which have in recent years been made in our streets, &c., evince that the laws under which we are now living are favourable to progress without disturbance of quiet. Report says that the Act which you are now asked to adopt has already earned some towns which have placed themselves under it, to regret their choice.

The Act makes no provision for enabling you to liberate yourselves from its evils after you have adopted it. *Now* you are free from its afflictions, *then* you will be powerless as slaves.

Do Not Surrender Your Freedom

Therefore be present in the **CORN EXCHANGE**, on the evening of the first **MONDAY** in **DECEMBER**, to give your unmistakable negative to the adoption of the Local Government Act, in Kettering.

A HATER OF THRALDOM AND WAST

November 1868

DASH, PRINTER, KETTERING

John Jenkinson was *A HATER OF THRALDOM AND WAST [Sic.].*
He and his "Economiser" friends won this battle.
It was not until 1872 that Kettering got a
Local Government Board

APPENDIX 10

A select list of John Jenkinson's publications

The Certain Salvation of all who Die in Infancy. Sermon preached at the new Baptist meeting, Kettering. London, Wightman & Cramp. Sold by the author, and Dash, Kettering, 1826.

A Letter to John Cooper Gotch, Esquire, containing a Reply to every Allegation advanced by the Rev. J. K. Hall, A.M., against the Author, 1828.

The Kettering Magazine, in manuscript form, 1828 to 1848.

Stanzas Occasioned By the Removal of the Sounding Board from Mr. Toller's Pulpit. A poem published as a folio handbill,1834.

A Letter to the Rev. George Bugg, A. B., Curate of Desborough, Northamptonshire. Containing a Summary of the Principles, Objects, and Means of Radicalism. By a member of the Kettering Radical Association, 1837.

Review of the Rev. A. Brown's Address.

Our Rights: or, The Just Claims of the Working Classes, stated, in a letter to the Rev. T. H. Madge, Curate of Kettering, by the Kettering Radical Association. J. Toller, Kettering & H. Hetherington, Strand, London, 1839.

The Duty of Christians to Abstain from all Appearances of Evil. A sermon preached at the Quarterly Meeting of Delegates of the South Midland Temperance Association held at Mountsorrel, Leicestershire, June 21st 1840. Sold by the Author, Kettering, Thomas Cook, Market Harborough, etc.

The Children's Farewell to Miss Chappell, late Mistress of the Girls' British School, Kettering on her leaving England for Jamaica, A poem. Toller, Printer, Kettering, 1840.

The Church and its Exactions; a Poem by John Jenkinson, Baptist Minister, Kettering, 1st August 1840.
(This provoked a riposte,*The Church and its Exactions. A Poem by John Jenkinson, Baptist and Chartist Minister, Kettering. Throughly* [sic.] *revers'd and refuted/truly reprov'd and corrected, by ITALICS.* Printed by the *Herald* Office in Northampton, 1840. A lampoon of Jenkinson's poem, with spoof publications, such as "Our Rights: or the Just Claims of the Seditious Classes.")

More Work for Italics. A Letter to the Rev. Henry Corrie, Rector of Kettering, by John Jenkinson, Baptist Minister, Kettering. Dash, Kettering, 1840. This brought *A Letter to John Jenkinson Anabaptist Minister Occasioned by his recent Address to the rector of Kettering.* Dash, Kettering, 1840.

The Altar of Testimony, a Copy of the Altar of Sacrifice. Sermon preached at the opening of the Baptist Meeting House, Spratton, J. Toller, Kettering, 1840.

Review of "An Address to the Parishioners of Isham Superior and Isham Inferior by the Rev. J. Mellor Brown, B.A., Rector", *containing Strictures on Mr. Brown's statements in reference to Infant Sprinkling; Sponsors; Dissent; Apostolical Succession; and Chartism by John Jenkinson, Baptist and Chartist Minister,* Sold by the author & J. Toller, Kettering, Winks, Leicester, etc., 1840.

An Address from the Members of the Kettering Temperance Association to the Visitors to the Town, at the Jubilee of the Baptist Missionary Society, Thomas Phillips, Northampton, 1840.

Ebenezer; or a Memorial of the Divine Goodness: addressed to the Church and Congregation Assembling in Ebenezer Baptist Chapel, Kettering, on the Completion of their Efforts for the Liquidation of the Debt incurred in the Erection of their Place of worship. Thomas Cook, Leicester, 1843.

Open Communion Indefencible: Or, remarks on a letter "Addressed by the Rev. W. Robinson To the members of the Baptist Church which meets in Gold Street, Kettering". By a STRICT COMMUNICANT. Northampton County Press, Printed by Westbrook & Isaac, 1843.

The Injustices of requiring Cottage Owners to pay Poor-rates for their Tenants. J. Ayer, Leicester, 1847.

A remarkable Answer to Prayer. Toller, Kettering. Undated poem published as a folio handbill. J. Toller, Printer.

Everlasting Love. Undated poem published as a folio handbill, J. Toller, Kettering.

Does Christianity Sanction War? B. L. Green, London, F. J. Barlow, Oakham, 1855.

The Universality and Unchangeableness of Jehovah's Laws. Poem by John Jenkinson of Oakham, Simpkin & Marshall, London, F. J. Barlow, Oakham, 1869.

In addition, Jenkinson wrote and published, (usually in the form of handbills) a number of works in verse, two of which are reproduced above. A number of these publications are to be found in the collections in Kettering Library and Northampton Central Library.

INDEX